Python-Powered Web Apps

A Practical Guide to Building Front-End Interfaces with HTML, CSS, and JavaScript

Thompson Carter

Rafael Sanders

Miguel Farmer

Contents

Chapter 8: Form Handling in HTML: Collecting Data from Users

Chapter 9: CSS Flexbox and Grid: Advanced Layout Techniques 210

Chapter 14: Security Best Practices in Front-End Development364

[27]

How to Scan a Barcode to Get a Repository

1. **Install a QR/Barcode Scanner** – Ensure you have a barcode or QR code scanner app installed on your smartphone or use a built-in scanner in **GitHub, GitLab, or Bitbucket.**

2. **Open the Scanner** – Launch the scanner app and grant necessary camera permissions.

3. **Scan the Barcode** – Align the barcode within the scanning frame. The scanner will automatically detect and process it.

4. **Follow the Link** – The scanned result will display a **URL to the repository.** Tap the link to open it in your web browser or Git client.

5. **Clone the Repository** – Use **Git clone** with the provided URL to download the repository to your local machine.

Chapter 1: Introduction to Web Development

Overview of Web Development

In today's tech-centric world, web development is the backbone of how businesses and organizations connect with users, facilitate interactions, and deliver products or services. Whether you're building an online store, a social media platform, or an enterprise-level application, the process of web development is fundamental in creating these systems. But before diving into the practical aspects, it's crucial to understand the core components that make up a web application: **front-end** and **back-end** development.

What is Front-End Development?

Front-end development is the part of web development that focuses on the **user interface (UI)** and user experience (UX). It's everything that users interact with directly in their web browsers. This includes layout, navigation, content, and any interactive elements that make up the look and feel of a website or web application.

Front-end developers use languages like **HTML, CSS**, and **JavaScript** to build the visual elements and ensure they are functional and accessible. Let's break down each of these technologies:

- **HTML (Hypertext Markup Language)**: HTML is the skeleton of any web page. It provides the structure and content, including headings, paragraphs, images, links, and other elements that make up the core of a website.

- **CSS (Cascading Style Sheets)**: CSS is the skin of the web. It controls the presentation, including fonts, colors, spacing, and layout. Without CSS, websites would look like plain, unstyled documents, making it essential for creating visually appealing designs.

- **JavaScript**: JavaScript is the language of interactivity. It allows you to create dynamic and interactive features on web pages, such as form validation, real-time updates, and other interactive behaviors. JavaScript is essential for modern web development and is increasingly used alongside front-end frameworks like React and Vue.js.

In short, front-end development is about designing and implementing what users can see and interact with in their web browsers. As the front-end is directly tied to user interaction, it's critical to ensure it is intuitive, responsive, and aesthetically pleasing. A poor front-end can result in user frustration, lower engagement, and even a loss of business.

What is Back-End Development?

Back-end development, on the other hand, refers to everything that happens behind the scenes. This includes the server, the database, and the applications that process the requests from the front-end. The back-end is responsible for managing and storing data, processing requests, and ensuring that everything on the front-end works smoothly.

Back-end development involves working with **server-side** technologies like:

- **Databases**: Databases are crucial for storing and retrieving data. Whether you're storing user information, product listings, or blog posts, a database is where your application's data lives. Common databases include **MySQL**, **PostgreSQL**, **MongoDB**, and **SQLite**.

- **Server-Side Programming Languages**: Back-end developers use programming languages such as **Python**, **Ruby**, **PHP**, **Java**, **Node.js**, and **C#** to create the logic that powers the application. These languages are responsible for handling the requests made from the front-end, interacting with databases, and sending data back to the front-end.

- **Web Frameworks**: Web frameworks simplify the development process by providing reusable components and structure for building web applications. Some popular web frameworks for back-end development include **Django** and **Flask** for Python, **Express** for Node.js, and **Ruby on Rails** for Ruby.

The back-end is invisible to users, but it ensures everything runs smoothly on the front-end. It's responsible for managing data, processing business logic, and ensuring that the user experience is as seamless as possible.

Full-Stack Development: Mastering Both Front-End and Back-End

While front-end and back-end development each serve different purposes, the intersection of both is what gives us **full-stack development**. Full-stack developers are proficient in both front-end and back-end technologies, enabling them to handle all aspects of building and maintaining web applications.

Why Become a Full-Stack Developer?

Becoming a full-stack developer provides a well-rounded skill set that can take your web development career to new heights. Here are a few reasons why mastering both front-end and back-end skills is essential:

1. **End-to-End Understanding**: As a full-stack developer, you can build an entire web application from start to finish. This includes everything from designing the user interface to

managing databases and handling server-side logic. This holistic understanding makes it easier to troubleshoot issues and optimize applications.

2. **Versatility**: Full-stack developers are versatile and can work on both front-end and back-end tasks. This flexibility is valuable for both small startups and large organizations. It means you can contribute to all areas of the development process, making you an invaluable team member.

3. **Career Opportunities**: Full-stack development skills are in high demand. Organizations are often looking for developers who can handle both the front-end and back-end, as it allows for a more streamlined development process. Full-stack developers are also often better equipped to understand and manage complex applications that involve multiple technologies.

4. **Better Collaboration**: Full-stack developers can bridge the gap between front-end and back-end teams. They understand both the client-side and server-side perspectives, which allows them to communicate more effectively with other team members and stakeholders.

While specializing in one area (front-end or back-end) is perfectly fine, being a full-stack developer enables you to work more independently and efficiently. It also gives you the opportunity to work on a broader range of projects, from small websites to large-scale enterprise applications.

The Tools of Full-Stack Development

As a full-stack developer, you need to be familiar with a wide range of tools and technologies. Here's a breakdown of what you need to get started:

- **Version Control Systems**: Tools like **Git** and **GitHub** allow developers to track changes in their code and collaborate with other team members.

- **Web Servers**: A web server is responsible for serving your web pages to users. Popular web servers include **Apache**, **Nginx**, and **Gunicorn** (for Python-based web apps).

- **Databases**: As mentioned earlier, databases like **MySQL**, **PostgreSQL**, **MongoDB**, and **SQLite** are essential for storing data and interacting with the back-end.

- **JavaScript Frameworks and Libraries**: On the front-end, tools like **React**, **Angular**, and **Vue.js** make it easier to build dynamic, interactive user interfaces. These frameworks and libraries help streamline front-end development.

- **Back-End Frameworks**: For the back-end, frameworks like **Django**, **Flask**, **Express**, and **Ruby on Rails** provide structure and tools for building web applications efficiently.

- **Cloud Platforms**: Cloud platforms like **AWS**, **Google Cloud**, and **Microsoft Azure** allow developers to host and scale their web applications. Full-stack developers should be familiar with these platforms to deploy their apps and manage infrastructure.

- **APIs**: Full-stack developers often work with **APIs** (Application Programming Interfaces) to enable communication between the front-end and back-end. APIs are essential for sending data between the client-side and server-side.

Setting Up Your Development Environment

Before diving into coding, you need to set up your development environment. This includes installing the necessary tools, frameworks, and libraries required to build web applications. Here's a step-by-step guide on how to set up your development environment for full-stack web development:

1. Installing Python

Python is one of the most popular back-end programming languages, and it's great for web development, especially with frameworks like Django and Flask.

- **Step 1**: Download the latest version of Python from the official Python website: python.org.

- **Step 2**: Install Python and make sure to check the box that says "Add Python to PATH" during installation.

- **Step 3**: Verify that Python is installed correctly by opening a terminal or command prompt and typing python --version.

2. Installing a Text Editor

You'll need a text editor to write your code. There are many excellent editors out there, but some of the most popular ones include:

- **Visual Studio Code (VSCode)**: A powerful, free, and lightweight editor with tons of extensions for web development. Download it from code.visualstudio.com.

- **Sublime Text**: A fast and simple editor with a sleek interface. Download it from sublimetext.com.

- **Atom**: A customizable open-source text editor. Download it from atom.io.

After installing your text editor, you'll want to install extensions for Python and web development, such as syntax highlighting, linters, and version control support.

3. Setting Up a Local Server

For testing your web applications locally, you'll need to set up a web server. Python comes with a built-in development server, but you can also use more robust servers like **Nginx** or **Apache** for production environments.

To start the built-in Python development server, navigate to your project directory in the terminal and run the following command:

```bash

```

```
python -m http.server
```

This will start a local web server that you can access by visiting http://localhost:8000 in your browser.

4. Installing Web Frameworks

Once your development environment is set up, you can start installing the web frameworks you'll be using for the back-end. For example, if you're using **Flask** for Python, you can install it with pip:

bash

```
pip install flask
```

For Django, the installation command is:

bash

```
pip install django
```

These frameworks provide the necessary tools to handle HTTP requests, route URLs, manage databases, and render templates.

5. Installing Front-End Tools

For the front-end, you'll need to install **Node.js** and **npm (Node Package Manager)**, which allow you to manage JavaScript libraries and frameworks.

To install Node.js, visit the official website: nodejs.org. Once installed, you can verify it by typing:

bash

```
node --version
npm --version
```

With Node.js and npm set up, you can install front-end frameworks like **React**, **Vue.js**, or **Angular** using the npm command. For example, to install React:

```
bash
```

```
npx create-react-app my-app
```

Real-World Example: How Companies Use Python for Full-Stack Development

To illustrate how Python is used in real-world full-stack development, let's look at some companies and projects that rely on Python for both the back-end and front-end.

1. Instagram

Instagram, one of the world's largest social media platforms, uses **Python** for its back-end services. The company relies on Python's simplicity, scalability, and wide range of libraries to handle everything from user management to content delivery. While Instagram's front-end uses JavaScript for dynamic features, Python powers the server-side logic, databases, and APIs.

2. Spotify

Spotify, a popular music streaming service, is another great example of a Python-powered application. The company uses Python for back-end services, including data processing and machine learning. Their front-end uses web technologies like **HTML**, **CSS**, and **JavaScript**, while Python handles the heavy lifting behind the scenes.

3. Pinterest

Pinterest is another tech giant that uses Python for full-stack development. Python is used for both the back-end (handling user data, image uploads, and recommendations) and in various machine learning algorithms that drive Pinterest's recommendation system.

Conclusion

Web development is a dynamic and essential field that combines creativity with technical skills. Understanding the difference between front-end and back-end development is crucial for becoming a well-rounded developer. Full-stack development is a highly valuable skill that enables you to build entire web applications from start to finish, empowering you to work on projects across both the front-end and back-end. By setting up your development environment and understanding the tools, you'll be ready to tackle real-world projects and develop the skills needed to succeed in web development.

Chapter 2: Understanding HTML: The Structure of Web Pages

What is HTML?

At the heart of every web page lies **HTML** (Hypertext Markup Language), the essential building block that provides structure to content on the internet. HTML is not a programming language—it's a **markup language**, designed specifically for creating and structuring content for the web. Think of HTML as the skeleton of a web page, providing the framework that everything else, including styling and interactivity, is built upon.

The Role of HTML in Web Development

HTML forms the foundational language of the web, working hand-in-hand with **CSS (Cascading Style Sheets)** for styling and **JavaScript** for interactivity. While CSS is used to control the look and feel of the web page, and JavaScript makes the page interactive, **HTML provides the structure**. Every piece of content you see on a webpage—be it text, images, forms, or buttons—exists because of HTML.

HTML is composed of **tags** and **elements**, each of which plays a specific role in the structure of the web page. It's crucial for any developer to understand how to use HTML to organize content in a way that is both logical and accessible, not just for users but also for search engines and web crawlers.

HTML as a Markup Language

In the world of web development, "markup" refers to the annotations in a document that describe how the content should be structured. When you're writing HTML, you're essentially marking up your content, telling the browser how it should be displayed. For example, you use HTML tags to define a **heading**, a **paragraph**, an **image**, or a **link**.

It's important to understand that HTML doesn't dictate how a page looks or behaves—that's where CSS and JavaScript come in. HTML's role is to organize and structure content in a way that makes it usable, readable, and accessible to both people and search engines.

HTML Tags & Elements: Introduction to the Most Commonly Used Tags

HTML documents are made up of various **tags**, and each tag serves a unique purpose. Tags are enclosed in angle brackets (<>), and most tags come in pairs: an opening tag and a closing tag. The content you want to mark up sits between these tags. Some HTML tags, like the <img> tag for images, are self-closing and don't require a closing tag.

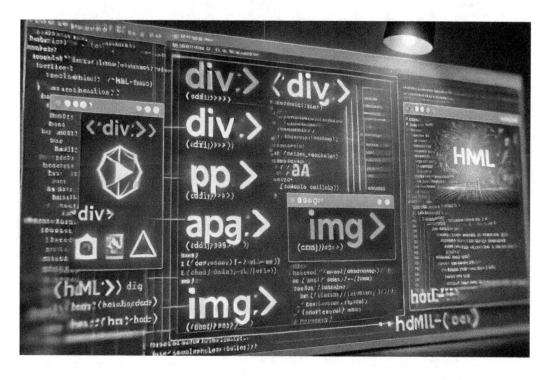

Let's take a look at the most common HTML tags used to structure a basic web page.

1. Document Structure Tags

The basic structure of an HTML document consists of a few foundational tags. These tags define the overall document and provide necessary metadata about the page.

- **<!DOCTYPE html>**: This declaration is used to tell the browser what type of document it's reading, ensuring that it knows this is an HTML5 document.

- **<html>**: This is the root element of the HTML document. Everything on the page, from headings to paragraphs to images, is contained within this tag.

- **<head>**: This section of the document contains metadata about the page, like the page title, character set, and links to external files (such as CSS stylesheets).

- **<body>**: The body tag contains all the visible content of the webpage—headings, paragraphs, images, forms, etc.

2. Text Tags

HTML offers various tags to structure text content, making it essential for structuring the body of your web page.

- **<h1> to <h6>**: These tags are used for headings. <h1> represents the largest heading (typically the title of the page), and <h6> is the smallest. Headings provide structure to your content and are critical for both user readability and SEO.

- **<p>**: This tag defines a paragraph. It is one of the most common tags in HTML and is used to group together blocks of text.

- **<strong>** and **<em>**: These tags are used for emphasizing text. <strong> is typically used to indicate important text (often displayed in bold), while <em> is used to emphasize text (usually displayed in italics).

- **<a>**: The anchor tag is used to create links to other pages, websites, or locations within the same page. It's essential for navigation and creating interactive content on the web.

3. List Tags

HTML supports both ordered and unordered lists. These tags are fundamental for organizing content in a list format.

- **<ul>**: This defines an unordered list, where list items are marked with bullets.

- **<ol>**: This defines an ordered list, where list items are numbered.

- **<li>**: The list item tag is used inside both ordered and unordered lists to define individual items.

4. Image and Media Tags

Images and other media content are an essential part of modern web pages. HTML provides a simple way to include multimedia.

- **<img>**: This tag is used to insert images into a page. The <img> tag is self-closing, and it requires the src attribute (which defines the path to the image) and the alt attribute (providing alternative text for accessibility).

- **<audio> and <video>**: These tags are used to embed audio and video files into your webpage, making it easy to integrate multimedia content.

5. Form Tags

Forms are one of the most important ways for users to interact with a website, whether it's for logging in, signing up, or submitting any other kind of data.

- **<form>**: This tag is the container for all form elements.

- **<input>**: The input tag is used to create form fields like text boxes, checkboxes, and buttons. The type attribute defines the type of input, such as text, password, radio, or submit.

- **<label>**: Labels are associated with form controls, providing accessibility and improving the user experience.

- **<select>** and **<option>**: These tags are used to create drop-down lists.

Structuring a Web Page: Organizing Content with Divs, Sections, and Containers

HTML provides a variety of structural elements that help organize content. These tags allow developers to create logical layouts and group related elements. While the <div> tag is the most commonly used, there are other elements designed for specific use cases that make structuring a page more efficient and semantic.

1. The <div> Tag

- **Purpose**: The <div> tag is a block-level container used to group elements together. It doesn't have any semantic meaning but serves as a "box" to hold content and apply styling. Developers often use the <div> tag to create sections of a page, like the header, footer, sidebar, or main content area.

- **Example Usage:**

html

```
<div class="container">
  <h1>Welcome to My Website</h1>
  <p>This is an example of a basic webpage
structure.</p>
</div>
```

In this example, the <div> tag is used to group the heading and paragraph together in a container that could be styled and positioned accordingly.

2. The <section> Tag

- **Purpose:** The <section> tag is a semantic element used to define sections of content, such as a header, footer, or article. It's more meaningful than the generic <div> and helps with both SEO and accessibility.

- **Example Usage:**

html

```
<section>
  <h2>Our Products</h2>
  <p>Explore our wide range of products.</p>
</section>
```

This tag is used to semantically indicate that the content inside is a distinct section of the webpage.

3. The <article> Tag

- **Purpose**: The <article> tag is used for self-contained content that could stand on its own, like a blog post or news article.

- **Example Usage**:

html

```html
<article>
  <h2>How to Build a Web Page</h2>
  <p>Follow these simple steps to create your own
website...</p>
</article>
```

4. The <header> and <footer> Tags

- **Purpose**: The <header> tag defines the top section of a webpage, usually containing the website's logo, navigation, and other introductory content. The <footer> tag defines the bottom section, often including copyright information, contact details, and links.

- **Example Usage**:

html

```
<header>
  <h1>Website Title</h1>
  <nav>
    <ul>
      <li><a href="#">Home</a></li>
      <li><a href="#">About</a></li>
    </ul>
  </nav>
</header>
```

5. The <aside> Tag

- **Purpose**: The <aside> tag is used for content that is tangentially related to the content surrounding it, such as sidebars or widgets.

Real-World Example: Building a Basic Webpage for a Fictional E-Commerce Store

Let's now apply our understanding of HTML to build a simple webpage for a fictional e-commerce store, which will include a header, a product section, and a footer.

Step 1: Setting Up the Basic Structure

html

```
<!DOCTYPE html>
<html lang="en">
<head>
  <meta charset="UTF-8">
  <meta name="viewport" content="width=device-width, initial-scale=1.0">
  <title>My E-Commerce Store</title>
  <link rel="stylesheet" href="styles.css">
</head>
<body>
```

```
<header>
  <h1>Welcome to My E-Commerce Store</h1>
  <nav>
    <ul>
      <li><a href="#">Home</a></li>
      <li><a href="#">Products</a></li>
      <li><a href="#">Contact</a></li>
    </ul>
  </nav>
</header>

<section class="products">
  <article>
    <h2>Product 1</h2>
    <img src="product1.jpg" alt="Product 1">
    <p>Price: $19.99</p>
    <button>Add to Cart</button>
  </article>

  <article>
    <h2>Product 2</h2>
    <img src="product2.jpg" alt="Product 2">
    <p>Price: $29.99</p>
    <button>Add to Cart</button>
  </article>
```

```
</section>

<footer>
  <p>&copy; 2025 My E-Commerce Store</p>
</footer>

</body>
</html>
```

This is the foundational HTML structure for a basic e-commerce website, with sections for navigation, products, and footer. The structure is straightforward and easy to adapt as your website grows.

Conclusion

Understanding HTML is the first step to mastering web development. It is the fundamental language that structures the web page and provides the foundation upon which all other web technologies are built. From basic text formatting to advanced structuring with semantic elements, HTML offers the flexibility and power necessary for building fully functional websites. By mastering HTML, you'll be equipped to build the skeleton of any web page and move on to styling and interactivity with CSS and JavaScript.

Chapter 3: Mastering CSS: Styling and Layout Techniques

What is CSS?

CSS (Cascading Style Sheets) is the language that brings life to web pages, taking raw HTML structure and transforming it into a visually appealing and user-friendly experience. While HTML provides the content and structure, CSS dictates how that content is displayed on the web. Whether you're designing the layout, choosing colors, or making the page responsive, CSS is your tool for controlling the look and feel of the site.

In its simplest form, CSS is used to **style HTML elements**—from text to images, buttons to forms—helping you create websites that are not just functional, but also aesthetically pleasing and easy to navigate.

The Role of CSS in Web Development

CSS is a powerful tool that allows web developers and designers to:

- **Control Layouts**: Arrange elements in a way that is visually pleasing and responsive to different screen sizes.

- **Enhance User Experience (UX)**: By controlling color schemes, typography, and spacing, CSS contributes directly to the overall feel of the website.

- **Make the Site Responsive**: CSS enables websites to adjust to various screen sizes, ensuring the site looks great on desktops, tablets, and smartphones.

- **Improve Performance**: With techniques like image sprites, CSS transitions, and animations, CSS can help optimize website performance while adding interactive elements.

At its core, CSS gives developers the flexibility to design and create visually stunning web pages. It's an essential skill for anyone working in web development and a key to creating modern, user-friendly websites.

Selectors, Properties, and Values: Understanding How to Apply Styles to Elements

CSS operates on a simple yet powerful mechanism involving **selectors**, **properties**, and **values**. These elements allow developers to pinpoint exactly which parts of a web page they want to style, and how.

1. Selectors: Targeting HTML Elements

CSS selectors are patterns used to select the elements on a web page that you want to style. Think of a selector as a set of instructions, telling the browser which HTML elements should receive a particular style.

- **Element Selector:** This targets all instances of a specific HTML tag. For example:

CSS

```css
p {
  color: blue;
}
```

This will turn the text color of all <p> (paragraph) elements to blue.

- **Class Selector**: This targets HTML elements with a specific class attribute. Class selectors are prefixed with a period (.). For example:

css

```css
.highlight {
  background-color: yellow;
}
```

Any element with the class highlight will have a yellow background color.

- **ID Selector**: This targets a single element with a specific ID. ID selectors are prefixed with a hash (#). Example:

css

```css
#main-header {
  font-size: 24px;
}
```

The element with the ID main-header will have a font size of 24 pixels.

- **Attribute Selector**: This targets elements based on the presence or value of an attribute. For example:

```css

input[type="text"] {
  border: 1px solid gray;
}
```

This applies a gray border to all <input> elements where the type attribute is text.

2. Properties: What You Want to Change

A property is a style feature that you wish to change. CSS properties control every visual aspect of an element, from the color and font of text to the positioning and layout of elements on the page.

Here are some common CSS properties:

- **color**: Changes the color of the text.

- **font-family**: Sets the font type for the text.

- **background-color**: Sets the background color of an element.

- **border**: Defines the border around an element.

- **padding**: Controls the space inside the border, between the border and the content.

- **margin**: Controls the space outside the border, between the border and adjacent elements.

3. Values: How You Want the Property to Be Displayed

Every property has a value that dictates how it should appear. Values vary depending on the property, but can include units like px (pixels), em, % (percent), or color codes such as #FFFFFF (hexadecimal) or rgb(255, 0, 0) (RGB).

For example:

css

```
p {
  color: #333333;
  font-size: 16px;
  line-height: 1.5;
}
```

In this example:

- color: #333333; sets the text color to a dark gray.

- font-size: 16px; sets the font size to 16 pixels.

- line-height: 1.5; sets the height of each line of text to 1.5 times the font size.

Understanding how selectors, properties, and values work together allows you to take full control of a web page's design and appearance.

Box Model and Layout: Mastering Margins, Borders, Padding, and the Content Area

One of the most critical concepts in CSS is the **box model**, which defines how elements are structured and how their dimensions are calculated. Every HTML element is considered a rectangular box, and CSS allows you to control the size and spacing of this box using the **box model**.

1. The Box Model: The Foundation of Layouts

The box model consists of four main parts:

- **Content:** This is where your actual content (text, images, etc.) resides.

- **Padding:** The space between the content and the border. Padding is used to create breathing room within the box.

- **Border:** The line surrounding the element, which can have different styles, widths, and colors.

- **Margin:** The space outside the border, which separates the element from other elements on the page.

Here's a visual breakdown of the box model:

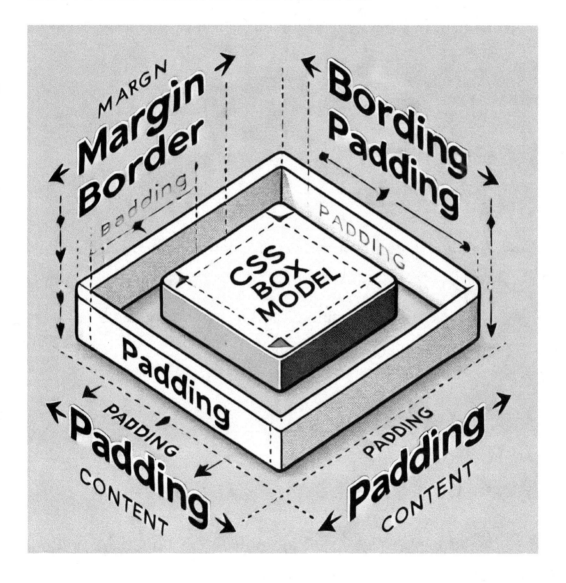

2. Understanding Each Box Model Component

- **Content:** This is the area where the text, image, or other content is displayed. You can control the dimensions of the content box using the width and height properties.

css

```css
div {
  width: 300px;
  height: 200px;
}
```

- **Padding:** Padding provides space between the content and the border. It's a useful way to ensure that content doesn't touch the edges of its container. Padding can be applied to all sides of the element or individually:

css

```css
div {
  padding: 20px;
}
```

You can also apply padding to individual sides (top, right, bottom, left):

css

```css
div {
  padding-top: 10px;
  padding-right: 15px;
  padding-bottom: 10px;
  padding-left: 15px;
}
```

- **Border**: A border surrounds the padding (and content). You can set its width, style (solid, dotted, dashed), and color:

css

```css
div {
  border: 2px solid black;
}
```

- **Margin**: Margin is the outermost layer, providing space between the element and other elements on the page. Just like padding, you can apply it to all sides or individually:

css

```css
div {
  margin: 30px;
}
```

3. Calculating Element Size: The Importance of Box-Sizing

By default, the total width of an element is calculated as:

```ini
```

```ini
width = content + padding + border + margin
```

However, you can modify this behavior using the box-sizing property to ensure that the padding and border are included in the width and height of the element.

```css
```

```css
div {
  box-sizing: border-box;
}
```

With box-sizing: border-box;, the width of the element is calculated as the width of the content, including padding and border. This makes layout calculations easier and more predictable.

Real-World Example: Creating a Simple Yet Stylish Homepage Layout

Now that we have an understanding of the fundamentals of **CSS**, let's put this knowledge into practice by creating a simple homepage layout for a fictional website. This will include a header, a main content section, and a footer, demonstrating how **CSS** works in the real world.

Step 1: HTML Structure

We'll start by defining the **HTML** structure of the page. This will include the header with navigation links, a content area with an article and a sidebar, and a footer.

html

```
<!DOCTYPE html>
<html lang="en">
<head>
  <meta charset="UTF-8">
  <meta name="viewport" content="width=device-width, initial-scale=1.0">
  <title>My Stylish Homepage</title>
  <link rel="stylesheet" href="styles.css">
</head>
```

```
<body>

  <header>
    <div class="container">
      <h1>My Stylish Homepage</h1>
      <nav>
        <ul>
          <li><a href="#">Home</a></li>
          <li><a href="#">About</a></li>
          <li><a href="#">Services</a></li>
          <li><a href="#">Contact</a></li>
        </ul>
      </nav>
    </div>
  </header>

  <main>
    <div class="container">
      <section class="main-content">
        <h2>Welcome to My Homepage!</h2>
        <p>This is a simple and stylish homepage
layout created with HTML and CSS.</p>
      </section>

      <aside class="sidebar">
        <h3>Latest News</h3>
```

```
        <ul>
          <li><a href="#">New Product
Launch</a></li>
          <li><a href="#">Upcoming Events</a></li>
        </ul>
      </aside>
    </div>
  </main>


  <footer>
    <p>&copy; 2025 My Stylish Homepage</p>
  </footer>

</body>
</html>
```

Step 2: CSS Styling

Next, we'll apply CSS to make this page look polished and well-structured. We'll use basic layout techniques like Flexbox to arrange the elements, and add styling to make it visually appealing.

```css
css

/* General Styles */
body {
  font-family: Arial, sans-serif;
```

```css
  margin: 0;
  padding: 0;
  background-color: #f4f4f4;
}


.container {
  width: 80%;
  margin: 0 auto;
}


/* Header */
header {
  background-color: #333;
  color: #fff;
  padding: 20px 0;
}


header h1 {
  margin: 0;
  font-size: 2em;
}


header nav ul {
  list-style-type: none;
  padding: 0;
  display: flex;
```

```css
  justify-content: space-around;
}

header nav ul li {
  margin: 0;
}

header nav ul li a {
  color: #fff;
  text-decoration: none;
  font-size: 1.1em;
}

/* Main Section */
main {
  display: flex;
  justify-content: space-between;
  padding: 20px 0;
}

.main-content {
  width: 70%;
}

.sidebar {
  width: 25%;
```

```css
  background-color: #fff;
  padding: 20px;
  box-shadow: 0 0 10px rgba(0, 0, 0, 0.1);
}


/* Footer */
footer {
  text-align: center;
  background-color: #333;
  color: #fff;
  padding: 20px 0;
}
```

Step 3: Testing the Layout

Once you've applied the CSS, load the webpage in your browser. You should see a clean and modern layout with a header, main content, sidebar, and footer. The navigation bar is horizontally centered, and the main content is displayed next to the sidebar using Flexbox.

Conclusion

Mastering CSS is crucial for web developers, as it controls the look and layout of every web page. From understanding the basic components like selectors, properties, and values, to mastering the box model and layout techniques, CSS is an essential tool that helps create visually appealing, user-friendly websites. By applying these techniques and principles, you can craft beautiful and responsive web designs that enhance the user experience.

In this chapter, we've laid the groundwork for CSS, including key concepts such as styling elements, understanding the box model, and creating modern layouts. With this knowledge, you're ready to move on to more advanced topics like Flexbox, Grid Layout, and responsive design, all of which will empower you to create complex and interactive websites.

Chapter 4: JavaScript Essentials: Adding Interactivity to Your Web Pages

What is JavaScript?

In the world of web development, **JavaScript** is a fundamental language that breathes life into static HTML and CSS pages, transforming them into dynamic, interactive experiences. While HTML structures the content and CSS designs the presentation, JavaScript governs the behavior of a webpage, allowing users to interact with the page in real-time. Whether it's form validation, dynamic updates, or even complex web applications, JavaScript is what makes websites come alive.

At its core, JavaScript is a **scripting language** that runs in the web browser. It allows you to respond to user inputs, manipulate the Document Object Model (DOM), and create features like dropdown menus, sliders, interactive maps, and real-time updates without needing to reload the page.

Unlike HTML and CSS, which are declarative languages used to define structure and style, JavaScript is an **imperative programming language**, meaning that it specifies the steps the browser must take to achieve a desired outcome. Whether you're adding form validation, creating animations, or manipulating data, JavaScript offers the tools you need to handle virtually any interactive element on the page.

JavaScript is also an essential part of **full-stack development** in modern web development, allowing developers to write both front-end and back-end code. On the front-end, JavaScript runs directly in the browser, while on the back-end, it can run on servers using technologies like **Node.js**.

In this chapter, we will break down the core concepts of JavaScript that every web developer needs to know. From defining variables to creating functions and working with loops, these essentials will provide a strong foundation for building dynamic web pages.

Variables, Functions, and Loops: Learn the Basic Building Blocks of Programming

Before diving into more advanced JavaScript topics, it's crucial to understand the basic building blocks that form the foundation of any programming language: **variables**, **functions**, and **loops**. These fundamental concepts allow developers to store and manipulate data, organize code, and repeat tasks efficiently.

1. Variables: Storing Data

In programming, a **variable** is a container for storing data values. JavaScript variables can hold many types of data, including numbers, strings, booleans, objects, arrays, and more. Variables are essential because they allow developers to store values and reuse them throughout their programs.

There are three main ways to declare variables in JavaScript: using **var**, **let**, or **const**.

- **var**: The old-school way to declare variables. Historically, var was used to declare variables in JavaScript, but it has some limitations when it comes to scoping.

javascript

```
var x = 5;
```

- **let**: Introduced in ES6 (ECMAScript 2015), let provides block-scoping, meaning the variable is only accessible within the block in which it is declared (e.g., inside a function or a loop).

javascript

```
let y = 10;
```

- **const**: Also introduced in ES6, const is used for declaring variables whose value will not change after being initialized (constants). It's best practice to use const unless you know the value will need to change.

javascript

```javascript
const z = 15;
```

Here's an example of how you might declare variables to store different types of data:

```
javascript
```

```javascript
let name = "John";    // String
let age = 30;         // Number
let isStudent = true; // Boolean
const pi = 3.14159;   // Constant
```

2. Functions: Organizing Code into Reusable Blocks

A **function** is a block of code designed to perform a specific task. Functions help organize code, make it reusable, and improve readability. You can define functions to carry out tasks like calculating a total, changing content on the page, or processing user input.

In JavaScript, you define a function using the function keyword, followed by the function name and parentheses. Inside the function, you can include a series of statements that will execute when the function is called.

```
javascript
```

```javascript
function greet(name) {
  console.log("Hello, " + name + "!");
}
```

```javascript
greet("John");   // Output: Hello, John!
```

In this example:

- greet() is the function name.

- The parameter name is a placeholder for the value that will be passed when the function is called.

- console.log() outputs the greeting to the console.

You can also create **arrow functions** (introduced in ES6), which are more concise and don't require the function keyword:

javascript

```javascript
const greet = (name) => {
  console.log(`Hello, ${name}!`);
};
```

```javascript
greet("Jane");   // Output: Hello, Jane!
```

3. Loops: Repeating Tasks Efficiently

Loops are used to repeat a block of code multiple times. They're particularly useful when you need to perform the same action on a list of items, such as displaying a series of elements or processing an array of data.

There are several types of loops in JavaScript, but the most commonly used are the **for loop** and the **while loop**.

- **for Loop:** The for loop is used when you know in advance how many times you want to repeat a block of code. You define the starting point, the condition for continuing, and the update step.

javascript

```javascript
for (let i = 0; i < 5; i++) {
  console.log(i);  // Output: 0, 1, 2, 3, 4
}
```

- **while Loop:** The while loop runs as long as the condition remains true. This loop is often used when you don't know in advance how many times the loop will execute.

javascript

```javascript
let i = 0;
```

```javascript
while (i < 5) {
  console.log(i);  // Output: 0, 1, 2, 3, 4
  i++;
}
```

- **forEach() Method**: The forEach() method is specifically designed for iterating over arrays. It's a cleaner way to loop through each item in an array.

```
javascript
```

```javascript
const arr = [1, 2, 3, 4, 5];
arr.forEach((item) => {
  console.log(item);  // Output: 1, 2, 3, 4, 5
});
```

These basic building blocks—variables, functions, and loops—are the core components of every JavaScript program. Mastering them will empower you to write dynamic, efficient, and reusable code for any web application.

DOM Manipulation: How to Change the Content and Behavior of Your Web Page Dynamically

The **DOM (Document Object Model)** represents the structure of an HTML document as a tree of objects. It allows JavaScript to interact with HTML elements dynamically, meaning that JavaScript can modify the content, structure, and style of a webpage after the page has been loaded.

When you manipulate the DOM, you can change text, add new elements, modify attributes, or even handle user interactions in real time. DOM manipulation is the backbone of building dynamic web applications that respond to user actions.

1. Selecting Elements

To begin manipulating the DOM, you first need to select the elements you want to interact with. JavaScript provides several methods to select elements from the DOM.

- **document.getElementById()**: This method selects an element by its ID.

javascript

```
const header = document.getElementById("header");
header.textContent = "New Header Text";
```

- **document.getElementsByClassName()**: This method selects all elements with a specific class.

javascript

```
const buttons =
document.getElementsByClassName("button");
for (let button of buttons) {
  button.style.backgroundColor = "blue";
}
```

- **document.querySelector()**: This method selects the first element that matches a given CSS selector.

javascript

```
const firstButton =
document.querySelector(".button");
firstButton.style.color = "white";
```

- **document.querySelectorAll()**: This method selects all elements that match a given CSS selector.

javascript

```
const allButtons =
document.querySelectorAll(".button");
```

```
allButtons.forEach((button) => {
  button.style.borderRadius = "5px";
});
```

2. Modifying Element Content and Attributes

Once you've selected an element, you can modify its content or attributes using JavaScript.

- **Changing text content**: Use textContent to change the text inside an element.

javascript

```
const heading = document.querySelector("h1");
heading.textContent = "Welcome to My Website!";
```

- **Changing HTML content**: Use innerHTML to change the HTML content inside an element.

javascript

```
const div = document.querySelector("#content");
div.innerHTML = "<p>This is a new paragraph.</p>";
```

- **Modifying attributes**: You can modify element attributes using setAttribute().

javascript

```javascript
const link = document.querySelector("a");
link.setAttribute("href", "https://new-link.com");
```

3. Adding and Removing Elements

You can dynamically add or remove elements from the DOM, making your webpage more interactive and responsive to user actions.

- **Creating new elements**: Use createElement() to create a new element, and then append it to the DOM.

javascript

```javascript
const newDiv = document.createElement("div");
newDiv.textContent = "This is a new div!";
document.body.appendChild(newDiv);
```

- **Removing elements**: Use removeChild() to remove an element from the DOM.

javascript

```javascript
const oldDiv = document.querySelector(".old-div");
oldDiv.parentNode.removeChild(oldDiv);
```

4. Event Handling

JavaScript can also be used to handle events like clicks, form submissions, and key presses. Event handling is crucial for creating interactive web pages.

- **Adding an event listener**: Use addEventListener() to listen for events and respond to them.

javascript

```javascript
const button = document.querySelector("button");
button.addEventListener("click", () => {
  alert("Button clicked!");
});
```

- **Removing an event listener**: Use removeEventListener() to remove an event listener.

javascript

```javascript
button.removeEventListener("click", myFunction);
```

Real-World Example: Building an Interactive To-Do List

Let's now build a simple yet interactive to-do list using JavaScript. This example will demonstrate how to apply everything we've learned so far—variables, functions, loops, DOM manipulation, and event handling.

Step 1: HTML Structure

First, define the basic HTML structure of the to-do list.

html

```
<!DOCTYPE html>
<html lang="en">
```

```
<head>
  <meta charset="UTF-8">
  <meta name="viewport" content="width=device-
width, initial-scale=1.0">
  <title>To-Do List</title>
  <link rel="stylesheet" href="style.css">
</head>
<body>
  <h1>My To-Do List</h1>
  <input type="text" id="new-task"
placeholder="Add a new task">
  <button id="add-task-btn">Add Task</button>
  <ul id="task-list"></ul>

  <script src="script.js"></script>
</body>
</html>
```

Step 2: CSS Styling

Add some basic styling to make the to-do list look better.

css

```
body {
  font-family: Arial, sans-serif;
  background-color: #f4f4f4;
  margin: 0;
```

```css
  padding: 0;
}

h1 {
  text-align: center;
  padding: 20px;
}

input {
  padding: 10px;
  margin: 10px 0;
}

button {
  padding: 10px;
  margin: 10px 0;
}

ul {
  list-style-type: none;
  padding: 0;
}

li {
  background-color: #fff;
  padding: 10px;
```

```css
  margin: 5px 0;
  display: flex;
  justify-content: space-between;
  align-items: center;
}


button.delete {
  background-color: red;
  color: white;
  border: none;
  padding: 5px;
}
```

Step 3: JavaScript Functionality

Now let's add the functionality with JavaScript to handle task creation, deletion, and marking tasks as completed.

javascript

```javascript
// Get DOM elements
const addTaskButton =
document.getElementById("add-task-btn");
const taskInput = document.getElementById("new-task");
const taskList = document.getElementById("task-list");
```

```javascript
// Add event listener to Add Task button
addTaskButton.addEventListener("click", addTask);

// Function to add a new task
function addTask() {
  const taskText = taskInput.value.trim();
  if (taskText === "") {
    alert("Please enter a task.");
    return;
  }

  // Create new task element
  const li = document.createElement("li");

  // Create task text node
  const taskTextNode =
document.createTextNode(taskText);
  li.appendChild(taskTextNode);

  // Create delete button
  const deleteButton =
document.createElement("button");
  deleteButton.textContent = "Delete";
  deleteButton.classList.add("delete");
  deleteButton.addEventListener("click", () => {
```

```
    li.remove();
  });
  li.appendChild(deleteButton);


  // Append the new task to the list
  taskList.appendChild(li);


  // Clear the input field
  taskInput.value = "";
}
```

Conclusion

JavaScript is the key to unlocking dynamic, interactive functionality on the web. It's an indispensable tool for modern web development, enabling you to manipulate the DOM, add interactive elements, and control the behavior of web pages. In this chapter, we explored the fundamentals of JavaScript—variables, functions, loops, and DOM manipulation—building a solid foundation for more advanced topics like AJAX, APIs, and frameworks.

By mastering JavaScript, you can create engaging, dynamic experiences that make your websites not only functional but also user-friendly and responsive to interactions. With the hands-on to-do list project, we saw how easy it is to add interactive features using simple JavaScript techniques. Keep practicing, and soon you'll be able to create fully interactive web applications from scratch.

Chapter 5: Integrating Python into the Web Development Workflow

---

1. Introduction: Python's Role in Modern Web Development

Python has surged in popularity over the past decade, not only in fields like data science, artificial intelligence, and automation, but also in **web development.** Its gentle learning curve, extensive libraries, and supportive community make Python an ideal choice for building everything from **small, single-page applications** to **large-scale, enterprise-grade websites**. While languages like JavaScript, PHP, and Ruby each have their own merits, Python has consistently proven itself as a robust, versatile, and maintainable solution for complex web projects.

In this chapter, we'll **explore Python's role** in web development by looking at the strengths of the language, comparing two of the most popular frameworks—**Flask** and **Django**—and diving into a real-world example of integrating a Python back-end with a front-end built on HTML, CSS, and JavaScript. By the end, you'll understand why Python is a powerful ally in any web developer's toolkit, and how to architect a web application that's both efficient and adaptable to changing business needs.

---

2. What is Python Web Development?

2.1. Why Python is a Great Choice for Web Development

Web development revolves around **efficiency**, **scalability**, and **maintainability**. Python excels in each of these areas:

1. **Efficiency:** Python's syntax is concise and intuitive, allowing developers to write features quickly. This results in fewer lines of code compared to many other languages, reducing development time and lowering the risk of bugs.

2. **Scalability:** From handling a few thousand daily visitors to running global-scale services, Python frameworks and libraries can scale to meet demand. Major companies like Netflix, Instagram, and Spotify rely on Python to handle millions of user interactions every day.

3. **Maintainability:** Python's emphasis on readability means that even large teams can work collaboratively on a project. The

language encourages clear, logical code structures, making long-term maintenance more manageable.

2.2. Versatility and Ecosystem

Python boasts an **extensive ecosystem of libraries**, frameworks, and tools that cater to a broad range of use cases, including web development. Whether you need to build real-time dashboards, create RESTful APIs, handle user authentication, or integrate machine learning models into your web application, Python's community-driven ecosystem has you covered.

- **Package Repositories:** PyPI (the Python Package Index) hosts hundreds of thousands of libraries, ensuring that if you have a problem to solve, chances are someone has already created a library to help you solve it quickly and reliably.

- **Cross-Platform Compatibility:** Python runs on Windows, macOS, Linux, and even embedded systems. This cross-platform nature makes development, deployment, and collaboration simpler, especially when dealing with teams using different operating systems.

2.3. Readability and Maintainability

Python is renowned for its **human-friendly syntax**. Code in Python often reads like pseudocode, making it easier for new developers to get up to speed and for experienced developers to maintain large codebases. This clarity significantly reduces both the learning curve and the cost of long-term maintenance.

Moreover, Python's emphasis on standard formatting (enforced by tools like **Black** or **PEP 8** guidelines) means that multiple developers can collaborate on a codebase without running into style conflicts. Over time, this consistency translates into fewer merge conflicts and a more streamlined development workflow.

3. Flask vs. Django: Choosing the Right Python Framework

3.1. Flask: The Lightweight Micro-Framework

Flask is often described as a **micro-framework** because it provides the essential building blocks for a web application without imposing a rigid structure. This minimalistic approach offers developers a great deal of **flexibility**. You can pick and choose the libraries and tools you need, tailoring the tech stack precisely to your project's requirements.

Key Features of Flask:

- **Lightweight Core**: Comes with a built-in development server, URL routing, and templating using Jinja2, but little else—making it easy to learn and extend.

- **Highly Customizable**: Since it doesn't dictate project structure, you can integrate libraries for databases, authentication, or form handling as you see fit.

- **Ideal for Small to Medium Projects**: Flask is perfect for prototypes, single-page applications, or modular microservices that need to remain agile and easy to modify.

3.2. Django: The "Batteries-Included" Powerhouse

Django takes a different approach, offering a **"batteries-included"** philosophy. It provides built-in features for common web development tasks—user authentication, ORM for databases, admin interface, form handling, and more. As a result, Django can help you rapidly develop complex applications without having to piece together multiple third-party libraries.

Key Features of Django:

- **Comprehensive Framework**: Provides most everything you need out-of-the-box, from URL dispatching to a robust ORM, authentication system, and even a production-ready administrative panel.

- **Convention Over Configuration**: Encourages best practices and design patterns, making your application more consistent and maintainable.

- **Ideal for Larger, Complex Projects**: With its highly structured approach and extensive built-ins, Django shines when building bigger systems that demand a robust, unified architecture.

3.3. Key Considerations When Deciding

Project Scope: For a smaller, experimental project or a microservice that requires a custom stack, Flask is likely your best bet. If you expect the application to grow into a massive platform with many features, Django's integrated tools will save you time and keep your architecture consistent.

Developer Experience: Flask's minimal approach is easier to start with, especially if you only need essential features. Django offers more guidance and best practices out of the box, which can be beneficial if you're working with a large team that needs consistent patterns.

Performance and Scalability: Both frameworks can scale well under high traffic if designed correctly. Flask might be slightly easier to scale horizontally because of its modularity. Django's integrated components, however, can streamline development for large applications that handle complex business logic.

---

4. Key Components of a Python-Powered Web Stack

Regardless of whether you choose Flask or Django, a Python web application typically includes several other layers and components. Understanding these pieces will help you build, maintain, and scale your project more effectively.

4.1. Virtual Environments and Package Management

In Python, **virtual environments** (often managed by tools like venv or virtualenv) create isolated environments for your project's dependencies. This prevents conflicting library versions between different projects on the same machine.

- **Creating a Virtual Environment**:

bash

python -m venv venv

source venv/bin/activate # On Unix systems

or venv\Scripts\activate on Windows

- **Package Management**: Use **pip** to install packages. Always keep a requirements.txt file or a pyproject.toml (for poetry) to track dependencies.

4.2. Database Options and ORMs

Your web application will likely need a database to store user data, session information, or content. Python supports a range of database solutions:

- **Relational Databases**: MySQL, PostgreSQL, or SQLite are popular for applications requiring ACID compliance.

- **NoSQL Databases**: MongoDB or Redis might be used for high-speed caching, analytics, or flexible schema requirements.

Frameworks often include an ORM (Object-Relational Mapping) layer that lets you interact with databases using Python classes and methods instead of raw SQL. Django comes with a robust ORM built-in, while Flask developers might opt for SQLAlchemy or Peewee.

4.3. APIs and RESTful Services

Modern applications frequently expose data through **RESTful APIs** or **GraphQL** endpoints. Python makes building these interfaces straightforward, whether you're using Django REST Framework (DRF) or Flask extensions like Flask-RESTful.

- **Django REST Framework**: Provides built-in tools for **authentication, permission handling, serialization**, and more.

- **Flask-RESTful:** A lightweight extension that makes building RESTful APIs intuitive without the overhead of large frameworks.

5. Real-World Example: Connecting Python Back-End to Front-End (HTML, CSS, JavaScript)

In this section, we'll walk through how to **connect a Python back-end** to a basic front-end. We'll start with Flask for simplicity, then outline how the example could be adapted to Django.

5.1. Setting Up the Project Structure

Let's imagine you're building a simple application called **"BookFinder"** that allows users to search for book information. The structure might look like this:

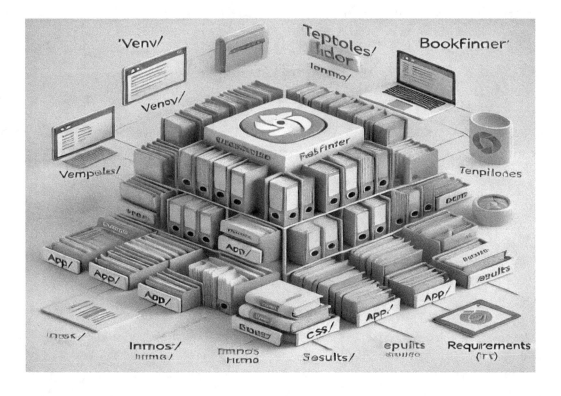

5.2. Creating a Basic Flask Application

In app.py, we'll configure a minimal Flask app:

python

```python
from flask import Flask, render_template, request

app = Flask(__name__)

@app.route('/')
def index():
    return render_template('index.html')

@app.route('/search', methods=['POST'])
def search():
    query = request.form['query']
    # For demonstration, we pretend to search a
database or API
    # In real scenarios, you'd connect to a
database or external service
    results = [
        {"title": "Learning Python", "author":
"Mark Lutz"},
        {"title": "Fluent Python", "author":
"Luciano Ramalho"}
    ]
```

```
    filtered_results = [r for r in results if
query.lower() in r["title"].lower()]
    return render_template('results.html',
query=query, results=filtered_results)


if __name__ == '__main__':
    app.run(debug=True)
```

Here's a breakdown of what's happening:

- **app = Flask(__name__)**: Instantiates the Flask application.

- **@app.route('/')**: The homepage is served via the index() function, which renders index.html.

- **@app.route('/search', methods=['POST'])**: Receives form data (query) from the front-end and processes it. In a real application, you'd query a database or external API. We then render results.html to display the filtered results.

5.3. Serving Dynamic Content and Templating

Flask uses the **Jinja2** templating engine. In templates/index.html, we might have a simple form:

```html
html


<!DOCTYPE html>
<html lang="en">
```

```
<head>
  <meta charset="UTF-8">
  <title>BookFinder</title>
  <link rel="stylesheet" href="{{
url_for('static', filename='css/styles.css') }}">
</head>
<body>
  <h1>Welcome to BookFinder</h1>
  <form action="/search" method="POST">
    <input type="text" name="query"
placeholder="Search for a book">
    <button type="submit">Search</button>
  </form>

  <script src="{{ url_for('static',
filename='js/main.js') }}"></script>
</body>
</html>
```

And for results.html:

html

```
<!DOCTYPE html>
<html lang="en">
<head>
  <meta charset="UTF-8">
  <title>BookFinder Results</title>
```

```html
    <link rel="stylesheet" href="{{
url_for('static', filename='css/styles.css') }}">
</head>
<body>
  <h1>Results for "{{ query }}"</h1>
  {% if results %}
    <ul>
      {% for item in results %}
      <li>
        <strong>{{ item.title }}</strong> by {{
item.author }}
      </li>
      {% endfor %}
    </ul>
  {% else %}
    <p>No results found.</p>
  {% endif %}
  <a href="/">Back to Home</a>
</body>
</html>
```

Notice how we use double curly braces ({{ ... }}) to **inject dynamic data** from our Python code into the HTML. This technique allows you to seamlessly blend front-end and back-end logic.

5.4. Handling Forms and POST Requests

In our example, we used a **POST request** to send the search query to the Flask app. The line request.form['query'] retrieves the value of the form input named "query". From there, you can process that data—search a database, call an external API, perform calculations—and pass the results back to a template.

5.5. Integrating Front-End Code: HTML, CSS, and JavaScript

Within the static folder, you can place all your **CSS** and **JavaScript** files. Flask provides the url_for('static', filename='...') function to correctly reference these static assets. For instance, in styles.css:

css

```css
body {
  font-family: Arial, sans-serif;
  background-color: #fafafa;
  margin: 20px;
}

h1 {
  color: #333;
}
```

And in main.js, you might have some client-side behavior, such as form validations, interactive elements, or fetch requests:

```javascript
document.addEventListener('DOMContentLoaded', ()
=> {
  console.log('JavaScript loaded');
  // Additional JavaScript code can go here
});
```

5.6. Extending the Example with Django

If you were to build a similar application in Django, you'd start by creating a new project:

```bash
django-admin startproject bookfinder
cd bookfinder
python manage.py startapp core
```

You'd then define views in core/views.py and map them in bookfinder/urls.py. Django's templating system is similar to Jinja2, but uses slightly different syntax and structures. Django also offers an **admin panel,** automatic handling of database migrations, and built-in user authentication if you need those features out of the box.

6. Building Scalable Architectures with Python

Once you've laid a solid foundation for your application, the next step is ensuring that it's **scalable, performant,** and **well-structured.** Python provides a suite of tools and best practices for achieving these goals.

6.1. Modularizing Your Codebase

For larger projects, organizing your code into **modules** and **packages** is critical. By breaking down functionality into clearly defined sections—such as auth, database, api, and templates—you make your application more maintainable and easier to navigate.

6.2. Handling Concurrency and Asynchrony

Although Python has a **Global Interpreter Lock (GIL),** frameworks and techniques exist for handling asynchronous or concurrent tasks:

- **AsyncIO:** Native to Python, allowing you to write asynchronous code using async and await keywords.

- **Celery:** An asynchronous task queue for running background jobs, scheduling tasks, or handling CPU-intensive workloads outside the main web process.

- **Threading or Multiprocessing**: Python's standard libraries for concurrency and parallelism, suitable for specific tasks that can benefit from parallel execution.

6.3. Microservices and Containerization

In modern software architecture, **microservices** are often deployed in containers (via Docker, Kubernetes, etc.) to provide flexibility, isolation, and scalability. Python is well-suited for microservices because frameworks like Flask can remain lightweight, focusing on a single responsibility.

A typical workflow might involve:

1. **Containerizing** each microservice using a Dockerfile.

2. Managing containers and scaling using **Kubernetes, Docker Swarm**, or **Amazon ECS**.

3. Ensuring each service communicates via well-defined APIs, typically REST or gRPC.

7. Security, Testing, and Deployment

7.1. Security Best Practices

Security is a top priority for any web application. Python frameworks like Django and Flask offer many safeguards, but developers must remain vigilant.

- **Input Validation**: Always validate data coming from user inputs to mitigate injection attacks.

- **Secure Credentials Handling**: Store secrets (API keys, database credentials) in environment variables or a secure key management system rather than hardcoding them.

- **CSRF Protection**: Use built-in CSRF tokens in Django or libraries like Flask-WTF to prevent Cross-Site Request Forgery attacks.

- **HTTPS Everywhere**: Serve your application over **HTTPS** to protect data in transit.

7.2. Automated Testing with Python

Automated tests ensure your application functions correctly and remains stable over time. Python's **unittest** and **pytest** are popular frameworks for creating **unit tests, integration tests**, and **end-to-end tests**.

- **Unit Testing:** Focuses on individual modules or functions.

- **Integration Testing:** Verifies that different parts of the application work together.

- **End-to-End Testing:** Mimics real user behavior through the entire stack, often employing tools like **Selenium** or **Playwright**.

7.3. Deployment Strategies

Once your Python web application is production-ready, you can deploy it to a variety of hosts or platforms:

1. **PaaS (Platform as a Service):** Services like **Heroku** or **PythonAnywhere** simplify deployment, automatically handling server configuration.

2. **IaaS (Infrastructure as a Service):** Services like **AWS EC2**, **Azure**, or **Google Cloud** give you more control but require you to manage servers, load balancers, and storage.

3. **Containerization:** Docker containers can be deployed to container orchestration platforms like **Kubernetes** or **Amazon ECS** for high scalability and reliability.

4. **Serverless**: Frameworks like **Zappa** or services like **AWS Lambda** can run Python functions on demand, removing the need for traditional server management.

---

8. Conclusion

Python has firmly established itself as a **cornerstone** of modern web development. Its clean syntax, rich ecosystems of frameworks, and supportive community make it an ideal choice for building applications of all sizes. Whether you opt for the minimalism and flexibility of **Flask** or the comprehensive, batteries-included approach of **Django**, you'll find that Python empowers you to work faster, write cleaner code, and adapt to changing requirements.

By integrating Python with front-end technologies like **HTML, CSS**, and **JavaScript**, you can build fully interactive, data-driven experiences. With careful consideration of security, scalability, and maintainability, you can create robust platforms that grow alongside your user base and evolving business needs.

In the chapters ahead, you'll delve deeper into topics like **responsive design, client-side interactivity**, and **advanced Python techniques**— continuing your journey toward full-stack expertise. Equipped with the foundational knowledge from this chapter, you're now prepared to harness the power of Python and bring your web development projects to life, whether you're crafting a personal project or contributing to the next big online sensation.

Chapter 6: Building Responsive Web Design with CSS Media Queries

---

1. Introduction to Responsive Web Design

1.1 Defining Responsiveness

Responsive Web Design (RWD) is an approach that ensures a website can adapt its layout and style to fit a variety of screen sizes, orientations, and resolutions. Whether viewed on a large desktop monitor, a tablet, or a small smartphone screen, a responsive site reflows its content in a way that remains easy to read and interact with. By using fluid layouts, flexible images, and **CSS media queries**, developers can deliver an optimal viewing experience that eliminates the need for users to pan, zoom, or scroll horizontally.

Historically, developers often created separate "mobile" versions of websites. However, this approach introduced complexity—maintaining multiple codebases, potential duplication of content, and redirect quirks. Responsive web design overcame these challenges by using a **single, cohesive set of HTML and CSS** that can serve every device.

1.2 Why Responsiveness Matters in Today's World

The world of digital content consumption has evolved drastically in the past decade:

1. **Device Diversity**: Phones, tablets, phablets, smartwatches, laptops, large-screen TVs—web experiences must adjust to a panoply of device types.

2. **Shifting User Behavior**: Users expect seamless browsing whether they're on the go or at home. Many visitors will leave a site quickly if they find it difficult to use on a particular device.

3. **SEO and SERP Importance**: Major search engines, including Google, factor mobile-friendliness into search rankings. Sites that aren't optimized for mobile risk losing visibility and traffic.

4. **Better ROI**: Companies that invest in responsive design often see higher conversion rates because potential customers can interact with content effortlessly, regardless of screen size.

1.3 The Philosophy Behind Mobile-First Design

A popular strategy for building responsive websites is the **mobile-first** approach. Rather than designing for large screens and then trying to condense everything down to fit smaller devices, developers start by crafting the simplest version of the site for mobile. From there, they progressively enhance the design as the screen size and capabilities grow. This method not only ensures a more efficient base style but also forces designers and developers to focus on **core content** and user tasks first.

Mobile-first typically means:

- Writing base styles (for small screens) that ensure the content looks good on devices with limited screen real estate.

- Using **min-width** media queries to add styles for larger screens.

- Ensuring performance remains a priority, since mobile connections might be slower, and devices can have lower processing power.

2. The Foundations of Responsive Layouts

2.1 Fluid Grids and Flexible Layouts

One of the cornerstone principles of responsive design is to **eschew fixed pixel widths** in favor of fluid grids. A fluid layout uses columns sized in relative units (like percentages, ems, or rems) instead of fixed pixels. This strategy allows the layout to adapt to the container it resides in.

Consider a three-column layout:

css

```css
.container {
  width: 100%;
  display: flex;
  flex-wrap: wrap;
}


.column {
  flex: 1 1 33.3333%;
  box-sizing: border-box;
  padding: 10px;
}
```

When the screen size shrinks below a certain threshold, these columns can stack vertically:

```css
css


@media (max-width: 768px) {
  .column {
    flex: 1 1 100%;
  }
}
```

By making your container and columns fluid, you enable the site to respond to varying screen widths dynamically.

2.2 Using Percentages and Relative Units

Relative units are a powerful concept in responsive design. **Percentages** automatically adapt to the parent container's width, making them integral for fluid grids. **Ems** and **rems** scale typography based on the font size of the parent element or the root element, respectively. This means when the user's default font size changes, or you set a different base font size for a particular breakpoint, text and spacing scale proportionally.

- **% (percent)**: Defines an element's size relative to its parent container.

- **em**: Defines size relative to the font size of the element's parent.

- **rem:** Defines size relative to the font size of the root HTML element.

Adopting these units helps maintain a consistent flow on your site, regardless of screen dimensions or user settings.

2.3 Responsive Typography

Responsive design isn't just about columns and images; typography also needs to scale. Large headlines can look overwhelming on tiny phone screens, while small body text might be difficult to read on high-resolution displays.

A simple technique is to set your base font size in **relative units**:

css

```css
html {
  font-size: 16px; /* Base size for most screens */
}


@media (min-width: 768px) {
  html {
    font-size: 18px;
  }
}
```

```
@media (min-width: 1024px) {
  html {
    font-size: 20px;
  }
}
```

By adjusting the root font size at specific breakpoints, all text throughout your site scales up or down appropriately, maintaining readability across devices. You can also tailor headings, subheadings, and body copy individually if you need finer control.

---

3. Anatomy of a Media Query

3.1 Understanding Breakpoints

Breakpoints are the specific screen widths at which your layout changes. Common breakpoints include 576px, 768px, 992px, and 1200px, corresponding to typical smartphone, tablet, laptop, and large desktop sizes, respectively. However, the best practice is to choose breakpoints based on your content's needs. If the text or layout starts looking cramped at 750px, set a breakpoint around that width.

3.2 The @media Rule: Syntax and Usage

CSS media queries rely on the @media at-rule, allowing you to apply styles only if certain conditions (media features) are met. A simple example:

css

```
@media (max-width: 768px) {
  body {
    background-color: lightblue;
  }
}
```

When the viewport width is **768px or less**, the background color changes to lightblue. Conversely, you can use min-width to target screens **768px or wider**. For a **range**, you can combine them:

css

```
@media (min-width: 768px) and (max-width: 1024px)
{
  body {
    background-color: green;
  }
}
```

3.3 Common Media Features (Width, Orientation, Resolution)

1. **width / height**: Targets the viewport's width or height. Often used for standard breakpoints.

2. **orientation**: portrait vs. landscape. Handy for tablets or phones that can rotate.

3. **resolution** or **device-pixel-ratio**: Targets high DPI screens like Retina displays. Typically written as @media (min-device-pixel-ratio: 2) or @media (min-resolution: 192dpi).

4. **prefers-color-scheme**: A relatively newer feature, letting you detect if a user's device is in light or dark mode.

3.4 Combining Multiple Media Conditions

Media queries can be combined using logical operators like and, or, and not. For example, to target both a minimum width and landscape orientation:

css

```
@media (min-width: 768px) and (orientation:
landscape) {
  /* Styles go here */
}
```

This approach gives you granular control over how and when certain styles should take effect.

---

4. Implementing CSS Media Queries in Practice

4.1 Setting Up a Mobile-First Stylesheet

A mobile-first strategy often places **universal base styles** (those that apply to small screens) at the top of the CSS, without any media queries. Then, you add additional media queries for screens of larger widths:

css

```
/* Base (mobile) styles */
body {
  margin: 0;
  font-size: 16px;
}

/* Larger screens */
@media (min-width: 600px) {
  body {
    font-size: 18px;
```

```
    }
  }
@media (min-width: 900px) {
  body {
    font-size: 20px;
  }
}
```

4.2 Handling Tablet and Desktop Breakpoints

As your design expands to tablets and desktops, consider how navigation, sidebars, and multi-column layouts will adapt. Key design elements to consider at each breakpoint might include:

- **Navigation Layout:** A simple hamburger menu for mobile transforms into a horizontal nav bar for desktops.

- **Column Count:** One column on mobile can expand to two or three columns on tablets or desktops.

- **Space for Ads or Secondary Content:** Additional screen real estate may allow including sidebars or extra widgets for desktop users.

4.3 Efficient Organization of Media Queries

To keep your code organized, you can group media queries near the relevant CSS rules or keep them in a separate file. Some developers prefer a **top-down** approach, where they write base styles first and place the media queries below. Others group everything for each component in one place. Both approaches are valid; the key is clarity for your development team.

Some tips for organizing media queries:

1. **Use Naming Conventions**: For example, prefix your classes with u- for utility, or create partial files that hold only media queries for certain breakpoints.

2. **Comment Rigorously**: Clearly label which breakpoint each media query targets.

3. **Avoid Too Many Breakpoints**: Only create new breakpoints when the design actually requires it. Over-segmenting your design can lead to complicated code.

---

5. Real-World Example: Converting a Desktop Site into a Mobile-Friendly Design

Nothing cements understanding quite like a practical example. Here, we'll transform a **desktop-centric layout** into a **mobile-responsive site** using HTML and CSS media queries. Let's imagine a fictional website named **"TravelExplorer,"** which showcases travel articles and photos. The desktop site layout currently looks like this:

We'll reshape this layout to ensure it's usable on mobile screens as small as 320px wide.

5.1 Project Setup and Overview

Assume the file structure:

Within index.html, we have the following simplified structure:

html

```
<!DOCTYPE html>
<html lang="en">
<head>
  <meta charset="UTF-8">
```

```html
  <title>TravelExplorer</title>
  <link rel="stylesheet" href="css/styles.css">
</head>
<body>
  <header class="main-header">
    <h1>TravelExplorer</h1>
    <nav class="main-nav">
      <ul>
        <li><a href="#">Home</a></li>
        <li><a href="#">Destinations</a></li>
        <li><a href="#">Tips</a></li>
        <li><a href="#">Blog</a></li>
      </ul>
    </nav>
  </header>

  <section class="content">
    <article class="featured">
      <img src="images/banner.jpg" alt="Beautiful mountain view">
      <h2>Escape to the Mountains</h2>
      <p>Experience the fresh air and scenic views of remote mountain destinations...</p>
    </article>

    <aside class="sidebar">
```

```html
    <h3>Sponsored Ads</h3>
    <p>Book your next adventure now!</p>
  </aside>
</section>

<footer class="main-footer">
  <p>© 2025 TravelExplorer. All rights
reserved.</p>
  </footer>
</body>
</html>
```

5.2 Step-by-Step Restructuring for Mobile Devices

Base Mobile Styles (No Media Queries)

We start with a **mobile-first** approach. By default, we'll stack elements in a single column:

css

```css
/* styles.css */

/* Base reset / basic styles */
* {
  margin: 0;
  padding: 0;
```

```css
  box-sizing: border-box;
}


body {
  font-family: Arial, sans-serif;
  line-height: 1.6;
  color: #333;
}


/* Header */
.main-header {
  background-color: #008080;
  color: #fff;
  padding: 10px;
  text-align: center;
}


.main-nav ul {
  display: flex;
  flex-direction: column;
  gap: 10px;
  list-style: none;
}


.main-nav a {
  color: #fff;
```

```css
  text-decoration: none;
  font-size: 1.1em;
  padding: 5px;
  background-color: #006666;
  border-radius: 3px;
}


.main-nav a:hover {
  background-color: #005555;
}


/* Content area */
.content {
  display: flex;
  flex-direction: column;
  gap: 20px;
  margin: 10px;
}


/* Articles */
.featured img {
  width: 100%;
  height: auto;
  display: block;
}
```

```css
/* Sidebar */
.sidebar {
  background-color: #f4f4f4;
  padding: 10px;
  border-radius: 5px;
}


/* Footer */
.main-footer {
  text-align: center;
  font-size: 0.9em;
  background-color: #008080;
  color: #fff;
  padding: 10px;
}
```

In this configuration, the header is centered, navigation links stack vertically, and the article plus sidebar are displayed in a single column. The site will look consistent on mobile devices without horizontal scrolling.

Introducing Breakpoints for Larger Screens

Next, we'll add media queries for tablets and desktops. Let's define two breakpoints: **768px** (common tablet width) and **1024px** (small desktops or large tablets in landscape).

css

```css
/* Tablet breakpoint: min-width 768px */
@media (min-width: 768px) {
  .main-nav ul {
    flex-direction: row;
    justify-content: center;
  }

  .content {
    flex-direction: row;
    gap: 20px;
  }

  .featured {
    flex: 2;
  }

  .sidebar {
    flex: 1;
    margin-left: 20px;
  }
}

/* Desktop breakpoint: min-width 1024px */
@media (min-width: 1024px) {
  body {
```

```
    max-width: 1200px;
    margin: 0 auto;
  }


.main-header {
  display: flex;
  justify-content: space-between;
  align-items: center;
  text-align: left;
}


.main-header h1 {
  margin-left: 20px;
}


.main-nav ul {
  gap: 20px;
  }
}
```

- **At 768px**:

  - The nav menu displays horizontally.

  - Content shifts to a two-column layout: the featured article takes up more space, while the sidebar is narrower on the right.

- **At 1024px:**

  - We center the layout with a maximum width of 1200px.

  - The header becomes a horizontal bar with the site title on the left and navigation on the right.

5.3 Optimizing Navigation, Images, and Typography

With the new breakpoints, the design is well-suited for mobile, tablet, and desktop. However, we can add extra touches:

1. **Responsive Navigation**: For smaller phones, consider a hamburger menu if your nav items exceed the space.

2. **High-Resolution Images**: Use srcset or the picture element to serve different image sizes for different devices.

3. **Fluid Typography**: Adjust base font sizes at each breakpoint to ensure comfortable reading.

css

```
@media (min-width: 768px) {
  html {
    font-size: 17px;
  }
}
```

```
@media (min-width: 1024px) {
  html {
    font-size: 18px;
  }
}
```

5.4 Testing Across Multiple Devices and Viewports

Testing is critical to ensure the site looks great on a variety of screens and orientations:

- **Browser DevTools**: Chrome, Firefox, Safari, and Edge all provide device emulators.

- **Real Devices**: Whenever possible, test on physical phones and tablets to catch any unexpected quirks.

- **Responsive Testing Services**: Tools like BrowserStack or LambdaTest help ensure consistent cross-browser performance.

6. Advanced Responsive Techniques

6.1 Retina Images and High-Density Displays

Apple's Retina displays, along with similar high-density screens on Android, compress more pixels into the same physical space. Images can appear fuzzy if not optimized. Techniques to handle this include:

- **Using 2x Images**: Provide higher-resolution images for screens with a device pixel ratio of 2 or more.

- **Vector Graphics (SVG)**: Wherever possible, use SVG for icons and logos since they are resolution-independent.

- **srcset and sizes Attributes**: Let the browser decide which image size to use based on screen width or pixel density.

Example:

```html
<img
  src="images/banner-1x.jpg"
  srcset="images/banner-1x.jpg 1x, images/banner-2x.jpg 2x"
  alt="Banner image"
/>
```

6.2 Responsive Video and Media Embeds

Videos, iframes, and other embedded media can break responsive layouts if they have fixed widths. One approach is to wrap them in a container with a responsive aspect ratio:

css

```css
.responsive-embed {
  position: relative;
  width: 100%;
  padding-top: 56.25%; /* 16:9 Aspect Ratio */
}


.responsive-embed iframe {
  position: absolute;
  top: 0;
  left: 0;
  width: 100%;
  height: 100%;
}
```

6.3 CSS Grid and Flexbox in Responsive Layouts

Modern CSS includes **Flexbox** and **CSS Grid**, both of which simplify the process of creating fluid, responsive layouts. For instance, a **CSS Grid** layout might look like this:

```css
css


.grid-container {
  display: grid;
  grid-template-columns: 1fr;
  gap: 20px;
}


@media (min-width: 768px) {
  .grid-container {
    grid-template-columns: 2fr 1fr;
  }
}


@media (min-width: 1024px) {
  .grid-container {
    grid-template-columns: 2fr 1fr;
    max-width: 1200px;
    margin: 0 auto;
  }
}
```

6.4 Progressive Enhancement vs. Graceful Degradation

- **Progressive Enhancement:** Start with a basic experience that works everywhere, then enhance the experience for modern browsers and larger screens.

- **Graceful Degradation:** Start with a fully featured experience for modern browsers, and then add fallback measures so older browsers or smaller screens can still function.

Both methods aim to ensure all users get a usable site, but progressive enhancement is often favored for responsive design because it naturally aligns with the mobile-first mindset.

---

7. Optimizing for Performance

7.1 Minimizing Render-Blocking CSS

When a browser encounters CSS files, it must parse them before rendering the page. Large or numerous CSS files can delay the **First Contentful Paint (FCP)**. Strategies to mitigate this include:

- **Minification:** Removing whitespace, comments, and unused code.

- **Bundling**: Combining multiple CSS files into one.

- **Critical CSS**: Inlining the CSS that's absolutely necessary for above-the-fold content, while deferring the rest.

7.2 Critical CSS and Lazy Loading

By extracting the CSS needed to render the first screenful of content and inlining it in the <head>, users see something almost immediately. The rest of the CSS can be loaded asynchronously. Similarly, large images or components not essential to immediate display can be **lazy-loaded**, so they only load when the user scrolls them into view.

7.3 Avoiding Layout Thrashing

Layout thrashing occurs when the browser recalculates a layout multiple times due to script or CSS changes. Minimizing DOM manipulations and using modern layout techniques (like Flexbox or Grid) helps reduce these recalculations and keeps your site performing smoothly across devices.

8. Testing and Debugging Responsive Designs

8.1 Using Browser DevTools

Chrome, Firefox, Safari, and Edge all offer **responsive design modes** within their DevTools. You can quickly switch between preset device sizes or even define custom dimensions. This preview can catch issues like:

- Horizontal scroll bars.

- Overlapping elements.

- Buttons and links that are too small to tap on touch devices.

8.2 Emulation Tools and Responsive Testing Services

Beyond DevTools, specialized services like **BrowserStack** or **LambdaTest** allow you to test real devices and multiple browser versions. This thorough approach helps ensure your site works seamlessly across different ecosystems, including older Android phones or less commonly used desktop browsers.

8.3 Common Pitfalls and How to Avoid Them

1. **Fixed Element Sizes**: Hard-coded widths in pixels can break your layout on narrower screens. Use relative units or max-width constraints.

2. **Overlapping Media Queries**: Conflicting rules can cause unpredictable results. Carefully comment and structure your CSS.

3. **Lack of Touch Optimization**: Interactive elements spaced too closely frustrate mobile users. Provide adequate spacing and consider using larger hit targets.

---

9. The Future of Responsive Web Design

9.1 Container Queries and Beyond

A much-anticipated feature in CSS is **container queries**, which allow components to adapt based on the size of their container rather than the viewport. This change will open up even more granular control, enabling truly modular, context-aware component design.

9.2 Dynamic Viewport Units

Recent CSS additions like lvh, svh, and dvh units help address issues with mobile browser chrome (the URL bar and UI). These dynamic viewport units can improve layout stability on mobile devices, eliminating the jumpiness when a browser's interface resizes the viewport.

9.3 Responsive Web Design in a World of Wearables and IoT

As technology expands to **smartwatches**, **smart TVs**, and other IoT devices, the principles of responsive design become even more crucial. Developers must think outside traditional breakpoints to accommodate voice commands, screenless interactions, or watch faces with unique circular displays.

---

10. Conclusion

Building a responsive website with **CSS media queries** is no longer a luxury—it's a necessity in an era dominated by smartphones, tablets, wearables, and ever-evolving screen technologies. By leveraging fluid grids, relative units, mobile-first CSS, and carefully chosen breakpoints, you can craft experiences that gracefully adjust to the user's device, bandwidth, and context.

From the foundational components like fluid layouts and flexible images to more advanced topics like retina optimization and CSS Grid, every aspect of modern web design hinges on responsiveness. Ensuring your site renders beautifully at all sizes not only improves usability and accessibility but also boosts your site's reputation, SEO ranking, and overall business impact.

Key takeaways:

- Adopt a **mobile-first** mindset to lay a solid base for smaller screens, then progressively enhance for larger viewports.

- Use **media queries** to apply device-specific rules, focusing on min-width or max-width breakpoints that cater to your content's natural reflow points.

- Don't forget about **performance**—lazy loading, minification, and critical CSS strategies help guarantee a swift and smooth user experience.

- Always **test across real devices** whenever possible, and use both manual and automated tools for thorough coverage.

As design trends evolve and new CSS specifications (like container queries) become mainstream, responsive web design will only grow more powerful and flexible. By staying current with best practices and continuing to test on new devices and interfaces, you'll be well-prepared to deliver accessible, elegant, and performant web experiences to users around the world—regardless of the device they choose.

Chapter 7: JavaScript Functions: Making Your Web App Smart

1. Introduction: The Power of JavaScript Functions

JavaScript is the driving force behind dynamic and interactive web experiences, and **functions** stand at the heart of that power. Functions enable you to break down complex tasks, reuse code, handle user events, and even shape the way your data flows throughout an application. In a language as flexible as JavaScript, functions take on additional, fascinating dimensions: they can be passed around like variables, returned from other functions, and even create their own enclosed "worlds" (closures) where data is kept private.

When you master functions in JavaScript, you open the door to building smarter, more modular, and more maintainable web applications. In this chapter, we'll explore everything from the basics—defining and calling a function—to advanced concepts like closures, higher-order functions, and real-time event handling.

We'll also walk through a **real-world example**: adding a "live search" feature that updates results dynamically as the user types. By the end, you'll be equipped to tackle more sophisticated UI behaviors and data manipulation patterns, all powered by JavaScript's flexible function model.

2. Defining Functions: Creating Reusable Code to Simplify Your Projects

2.1 What Are Functions?

A function is a **reusable block of code** designed to perform a particular task. Functions can accept input in the form of parameters, process data, and return output. This modular approach keeps your code organized and adaptable. Rather than writing the same logic multiple times, you define a function once and call it whenever needed. This fosters the **DRY principle** (Don't Repeat Yourself), reducing the risk of errors and making your code easier to maintain.

2.2 Anatomy of a Function Declaration

In JavaScript, one common way to define a function is through a **function declaration**:

```javascript
```

```javascript
function greetUser(name) {
  console.log("Hello, " + name + "!");
}
```

Here's the breakdown:

1. **Keyword**: function signifies that we're creating a new function.

2. **Function Name**: greetUser is the identifier we use to call this function later.

3. **Parameters**: (name) is a list of variables that the function will receive from the caller.

4. **Function Body**: The code inside { ... } performs the function's task—in this case, logging a greeting message to the console.

To use greetUser, we call it:

```javascript
```

```javascript
greetUser("Alice"); // Logs: "Hello, Alice!"
greetUser("Bob");   // Logs: "Hello, Bob!"
```

By wrapping this behavior in a function, you can greet any user by name without duplicating the same console log logic across your codebase.

2.3 Function Expressions

Another popular way to define a function is via a **function expression**:

javascript

```javascript
const greetUser = function (name) {
  console.log("Hello, " + name + "!");
};
```

Differences between function declarations and function expressions:

- Function **declarations** are hoisted to the top of their scope, meaning you can call them before they're defined in your code.

- Function **expressions** are assigned to a variable at runtime, so you can only call them after that line is executed.

Developers often prefer function expressions for their clarity—it's easier to see the exact point in the code where the function is created, and expressions can integrate seamlessly with arrow functions and callback patterns.

2.4 Arrow Functions and Lexical this

Introduced in ES6, **arrow functions** provide a shorter syntax and a lexical binding of this. Here's a simple arrow function:

```javascript
const greetUser = (name) => {
  console.log(`Hello, ${name}!`);
};
```

Notable points about arrow functions:

- If your function body has a single statement and returns a value, you can omit the { ... } and return keyword:

```javascript
const add = (a, b) => a + b;
```

- Arrow functions do **not** create their own this context. Instead, they inherit the this from the parent scope. This is especially useful in scenarios like class methods or callbacks where you want to maintain the outer context.

Despite their brevity, arrow functions are not a complete replacement for traditional functions. They **cannot** be used as constructors (you can't use new with them) and they have no prototype. However, for most modern JavaScript use cases—like event callbacks or array manipulations—arrow functions often provide a cleaner approach.

2.5 Best Practices for Naming and Structuring Functions

- **Use Meaningful Names:** A well-chosen name such as calculateInvoiceTotal is far more expressive than calcIt.

- **Limit the Number of Parameters:** Accept too many parameters, and your function becomes unwieldy. Consider using an object or destructuring if a function needs more than three or four parameters.

- **Keep Functions Small:** Each function should do one thing well—if you find a single function doing multiple unrelated tasks, it's probably time to split it.

- **Document Your Functions:** Even with good naming conventions, a short doc comment explaining inputs and outputs helps other developers (and your future self) quickly understand the code.

3. Advanced Function Techniques

Once you've got the basics down, JavaScript functions open up a world of **advanced patterns**. Let's explore some that will further elevate your code.

3.1 Higher-Order Functions

A **higher-order function** is any function that either:

1. Accepts functions as arguments, or

2. Returns a function.

In JavaScript, functions are **first-class citizens**, meaning you can pass them around just like any other data type. For instance, consider this array helper that takes a function to test each element:

```javascript
function filterArray(arr, testFunc) {
  const results = [];
  for (const item of arr) {
    if (testFunc(item)) {
      results.push(item);
    }
  }
  return results;
}
```

```
const numbers = [1, 2, 3, 4, 5];
const evenNumbers = filterArray(numbers, (num) =>
num % 2 === 0);
```

```
console.log(evenNumbers); // [2, 4]
```

Here, filterArray is a higher-order function because it receives another function (testFunc) as a parameter. This design pattern is extremely powerful, as it decouples the iteration logic from the condition used to determine if items pass a test.

3.2 Callback Functions and Asynchronous Patterns

In web development, you frequently need to perform tasks that take time—like fetching data over a network. JavaScript uses an **asynchronous** model to handle these tasks without freezing the main thread. One of the fundamental tools in this model is the **callback function**.

A typical callback-based function might look like this:

```
javascript
```

```
function getData(url, callback) {
  const xhr = new XMLHttpRequest();
```

```
xhr.open("GET", url);
xhr.onload = () => {
  if (xhr.status === 200) {
    callback(null, xhr.responseText);
  } else {
    callback(new Error("Request failed"));
  }
};
xhr.send();
}


getData("https://api.example.com/data", (err,
data) => {
  if (err) {
    console.error("Error fetching data:", err);
  } else {
    console.log("Data received:", data);
  }
});
```

While callback functions are effective, they can lead to **callback hell** if you have multiple asynchronous steps in sequence. Modern JavaScript often uses **Promises** and **async/await** as a more elegant solution, but understanding callbacks is still critical.

3.3 Immediately Invoked Function Expressions (IIFEs)

An **IIFE** (pronounced "iffy") is a function that's defined and executed immediately. This pattern was historically used to create **private scopes** in JavaScript—helpful back when JavaScript didn't have block-scope variables (let and const):

javascript

```
(function () {
  const privateVar = "I am private";
  console.log("IIFE executed!");
})();
```

Although ES6 modules and block-scoped variables have largely replaced IIFEs, you might still see them in legacy code or specialized scenarios. They can also be used for **module patterns**, bundling related functions and data into a single scope.

3.4 Closures and Encapsulation

A **closure** is created when an inner function references variables from an outer function, even after the outer function has returned. This feature allows private data and methods in JavaScript:

javascript

```javascript
function createCounter() {
  let count = 0;
  return function () {
    count++;
    return count;
  };
}


const counterA = createCounter();
console.log(counterA()); // 1
console.log(counterA()); // 2

const counterB = createCounter();
console.log(counterB()); // 1
```

Each call to createCounter() returns a function that has access to its own count variable, and the data is kept private—outside code cannot directly manipulate count. Closures enable advanced patterns like memoization, partial application, and encapsulation without classical classes.

4. Event Listeners and Handlers: Triggering Functions Based on User Actions

Interactivity in web applications arises through **events**—clicks, keypresses, scrolls, and more. JavaScript listens for these events and responds with functions called **event handlers**.

4.1 The DOM Event Model

Modern browsers use the **DOM Level 2** event model, which provides:

- **Event Target:** The element on which the event occurs.

- **Capturing Phase:** Events travel from the window down through ancestor elements.

- **Targeting Phase:** The event arrives at the element that triggered it.

- **Bubbling Phase:** The event "bubbles up" from the target element back through its ancestors, potentially triggering more handlers.

4.2 addEventListener() vs. Inline Event Handlers

There are multiple ways to bind an event handler in JavaScript:

1. Inline HTML attributes:

html

```html
<button onclick="alert('Clicked!')">Click Me</button>
```

This approach mixes HTML and JavaScript, which can become messy in larger projects.

2. The old-school onEvent property:

javascript

```javascript
const btn = document.getElementById("myButton");
btn.onclick = function () {
  alert("Clicked!");
};
```

This approach is more maintainable but still limited (assigning a second handler overwrites the first).

3. Modern addEventListener():

javascript

```javascript
const btn = document.getElementById("myButton");
btn.addEventListener("click", () => {
  alert("Clicked!");
});
```

This is the recommended method. It lets you register multiple listeners for the same event and cleanly remove them later if necessary.

4.3 Event Propagation: Capturing, Targeting, and Bubbling

Consider a nested structure:

html

```html
<div id="parent">
  <button id="child">Click Me</button>
</div>
```

When the user clicks the button:

1. The event travels from window → document → <html> → <body> → #parent → #child during **capturing**.

2. The event is **targeted** at #child.

3. Then it **bubbles** back up: #child → #parent → <body> → <html> → document → window.

Using addEventListener() with the third optional argument true sets a listener in the capturing phase, while omitting it or using false sets a listener in the bubbling phase.

4.4 Removing Event Listeners

To remove an event listener, pass the same **function reference** and **options** you used when adding it:

```javascript
function handleClick() {
  alert("Button clicked!");
}


const btn = document.getElementById("myButton");
btn.addEventListener("click", handleClick);


// Remove the listener
btn.removeEventListener("click", handleClick);
```

Anonymous (inline) functions can't be removed because there's no reference to them stored.

4.5 Common Event Types and Use Cases

- **Click Events**: Buttons, links, and interactive elements.

- **Keyboard Events**: Form validation, shortcuts, or game controls using keydown, keypress, and keyup.

- **Mouse Events**: Hover behavior with mouseover and mouseout, drag-and-drop with dragstart, dragover, drop.

- **Touch Events** (mobile devices): touchstart, touchmove, touchend.

- **Window Events**: resize, scroll, and DOMContentLoaded for adjusting layout or lazy-loading content.

---

5. Real-World Example: Implementing a Live Search Bar with JavaScript

Nothing cements understanding like a practical, hands-on project. Let's walk through **building a live search bar**—a feature that updates displayed search results as soon as the user starts typing. This functionality is common in e-commerce sites, blogs, and social platforms, where quick search feedback is crucial for good user experience.

5.1 Project Overview and Setup

Imagine a simple HTML page that displays a list of items (e.g., products, articles, or user profiles). The user can type into a search field, and the page immediately filters the visible items based on what they typed, without needing a page reload.

We'll focus on these key aspects:

1. **HTML Structure**: A text input for searching and a container with items.

2. **JavaScript**:

   o Capturing the input event on the search field.

   o Filtering or highlighting items in real time.

3. **(Optional) Styling**: Use CSS to make the search bar look sleek, but we'll focus primarily on functionality.

5.2 Designing the HTML Markup for a Search Component

Here's a basic HTML scaffold:

html

```
<!DOCTYPE html>
<html lang="en">
<head>
  <meta charset="UTF-8">
  <title>Live Search Example</title>
  <link rel="stylesheet" href="styles.css">
</head>
<body>
  <h1>Live Search Demo</h1>
  <div class="search-container">
    <input type="text" id="search-input"
placeholder="Type to search...">
  </div>

  <ul id="item-list">
    <li>Banana</li>
    <li>Apple</li>
    <li>Avocado</li>
    <li>Blueberry</li>
    <li>Cherry</li>
    <li>Mango</li>
    <li>Pineapple</li>
  </ul>

  <script src="script.js"></script>
```

```
</body>
</html>
```

- **<input>**: The text field where the user enters a search term.

- **<ul>**: Contains list items for demonstration (Banana, Apple, etc.). In a real-world application, this data might come from an API or database.

5.3 Connecting the Front-End to a Data Source

In many production scenarios, the items would be fetched from a back-end service or loaded dynamically. For this example, we're using a static list. If you wanted to load data from an API, you could:

javascript

```javascript
async function fetchItems() {
  try {
    const response = await
fetch('https://example.com/items.json');
    const items = await response.json();
    // Render items on the page
  } catch (err) {
    console.error('Error fetching items:', err);
  }
}
```

But let's keep it simple by just selecting the existing <li> elements in our DOM.

5.4 Leveraging Event Listeners for Instant Feedback

script.js:

```javascript

// Step 1: Grab references to DOM elements
const searchInput =
document.getElementById("search-input");
const itemList = document.getElementById("item-list");
const items = itemList.getElementsByTagName("li");

// Step 2: Add an event listener to the search field
searchInput.addEventListener("input",
handleSearch);

function handleSearch() {
  const query =
searchInput.value.toLowerCase().trim();

  for (let i = 0; i < items.length; i++) {
```

```
    const itemText =
items[i].textContent.toLowerCase();

    if (itemText.includes(query)) {
      items[i].style.display = "list-item";
    } else {
      items[i].style.display = "none";
    }
  }
}
```

Explanation:

1. **searchInput.addEventListener("input", handleSearch);:** The "input" event fires every time the user types, deletes, or modifies the text.

2. **handleSearch()** reads the current input value, then compares it to each item's text.

3. If the item text includes the search query, the item remains visible (display = "list-item"). Otherwise, we hide it (display = "none").

This approach is fast enough for small sets of data. If you have hundreds or thousands of items, consider more efficient searching algorithms or a server-side search endpoint.

5.5 Throttling or Debouncing for Performance

In many real-world apps, you don't want the search function to run on every single keystroke—especially if each search triggers a network request. Techniques like **debouncing** or **throttling** help by limiting how often a function fires:

- **Debounce**: Delays the function until the user stops typing for a certain period (e.g., 300ms).

- **Throttle**: Allows the function to run at a maximum rate (e.g., once every 200ms) regardless of how fast the user types.

A debounce example:

javascript

```javascript
function debounce(func, delay) {
  let timeout;
  return function (...args) {
    clearTimeout(timeout);
    timeout = setTimeout(() => func.apply(this,
args), delay);
  };
}

const debouncedSearch = debounce(handleSearch,
300);
```

```
searchInput.addEventListener("input",
debouncedSearch);
```

Now, handleSearch() will only execute if the user hasn't typed for 300ms, reducing unnecessary calls.

5.6 Enhancing the Search with Highlighting and Auto-Suggestions

To provide an even more user-friendly experience, consider:

- **Highlighting Matches**: Wrap matching text in <span> tags with a highlight CSS class.

- **Auto-Suggestions**: Show a dropdown list of suggestions as the user types, and let them navigate using arrow keys or mouse clicks.

- **Category Filters**: If items belong to categories (e.g., fruits, vegetables), you could show grouped search results or checkboxes to refine the search.

Example snippet for highlighting:

```javascript
function highlightText(text, query) {
  const index =
text.toLowerCase().indexOf(query.toLowerCase());
```

```
if (index === -1) return text;

  const match = text.substring(index, index +
query.length);
  return text.substring(0, index) + "<span
class='highlight'>" +
        match + "</span>" + text.substring(index
+ query.length);
}
```

You would then inject this HTML into the page (carefully sanitized or validated) instead of setting textContent.

5.7 Testing and Debugging the Live Search Feature

1. **Check Edge Cases**: What if the search is empty? Make sure all items show.

2. **Case Sensitivity**: By lowercasing everything, we perform a **case-insensitive** search.

3. **Special Characters**: Users might type non-alphanumeric characters. Decide how to handle them.

4. **Performance**: On large data sets, confirm the UI remains smooth. If not, optimize or consider server-based searching.

5. **Responsive Behavior**: Ensure the search bar and results look good on mobile devices.

---

6. Error Handling and Debugging Functions

When building sophisticated web apps, functions can fail due to **logic errors, unexpected inputs, or external issues** like network timeouts. A robust approach to error handling ensures your program can recover gracefully or provide meaningful feedback.

6.1 Common Function-Related Bugs

- **Parameter Mismatch**: JavaScript won't stop you from calling a function with too few or too many arguments. In some cases, this can lead to undefined references or odd behaviors if you rely on a missing argument.

- **Scope and Shadowing**: Redeclaring a variable in an inner scope can shadow a variable in an outer scope, leading to unintended side effects.

- **This Binding**: Using the wrong type of function or losing context can cause this to become undefined. This is particularly common in event handlers.

6.2 Using console.log() and Breakpoints

- **console.log()**: Inserting console.log() statements can help you see what's happening at various stages of a function.

- **DevTools Breakpoints**: Most browsers allow you to set breakpoints in your JavaScript code, pausing execution to inspect variable states line by line.

6.3 Defensive Programming and Validation

- **Check Input Types**: If a function expects a number, confirm that the argument is indeed numeric.

- **Guard Clauses**: If something is missing or invalid, bail out early:

```javascript
function processUserInput(user) {
  if (!user || !user.name) {
    console.error("Invalid user object");
    return;
  }
  // continue with processing
}
```

- **Try/Catch Blocks**: For code that might throw exceptions—like JSON parsing or network requests—wrap it in a try/catch to handle errors gracefully.

---

7. Performance Considerations

7.1 Minimizing Global Lookups

Each time you access a global variable (like window or document) or a deeply nested object property, JavaScript has to search the scope chain. A minor optimization is to store references locally:

javascript

```
const doc = document;
const heading = doc.getElementById("heading");
```

While micro-optimizations are rarely the key to major performance gains, they can matter in code that runs extremely frequently (e.g., inside animations or large loops).

7.2 Function Scope and Memory Usage

If a function retains references to large objects in closures, you could inadvertently keep significant portions of memory alive. Be mindful about creating closures that store large arrays, DOM nodes, or other memory-heavy data when they're no longer needed.

7.3 Caching and Memoization

Memoization stores the results of function calls so you don't compute them again with the same inputs. Useful in scenarios like repeated calculations or transformations:

javascript

```javascript
function memoize(fn) {
  const cache = {};
  return function (...args) {
    const key = JSON.stringify(args);
    if (cache[key]) {
      return cache[key];
    }
    const result = fn(...args);
    cache[key] = result;
    return result;
  };
}


function expensiveOperation(num) {
  // Some CPU-intensive process
  return num ** 3;
}
```

```
const memoizedOperation =
memoize(expensiveOperation);
console.log(memoizedOperation(10)); // Calculated,
then cached
console.log(memoizedOperation(10)); // Returned
from cache
```

7.4 Best Practices for Event-Driven Apps

- **Detach Unneeded Event Handlers**: If a DOM element is removed, also remove associated event listeners to avoid memory leaks.

- **Use Delegation**: In lists or tables with many child elements, attach an event listener to a parent node. Let the event **bubble** up to the parent and handle it there, reducing the overhead of attaching separate listeners to each child.

---

8. Security Implications of JavaScript Functions

JavaScript can be a vector for **Cross-Site Scripting (XSS)**, especially if you're injecting user-supplied content into the DOM without sanitizing it first. Functions that handle or transform user input must do so carefully.

8.1 Avoiding Common Security Pitfalls

- **Never eval() Untrusted Strings**: eval() executes a string of JavaScript code, opening the door to malicious scripts.

- **Escape Output**: When inserting text into the DOM, consider using textContent or relevant escaping techniques.

- **Validate Inputs**: Filter or sanitize data at the server level and re-check them in the client if needed.

8.2 Sanitizing User Input

If your web app allows user-generated content (like a comment or message board), leverage libraries (e.g., DOMPurify) or server-side sanitization. Even if your code is well-structured, user content can contain malicious <script> tags or event attributes that run unexpectedly.

8.3 Safely Handling External APIs

When dealing with external APIs, especially ones returning HTML or script data, treat them with caution. Use **Content Security Policy (CSP)** headers, ensure you trust the source, and parse or sanitize the data if you're inserting it into the DOM.

9. Future Trends and Conclusion

9.1 The Evolution of JavaScript Functions (Async/Await, Generators)

JavaScript continues to evolve. Functions got an incredible boost with ES6 and beyond:

- **Promises**: Provide a better pattern over callbacks for async flows.

- **async/await**: Let you write asynchronous code that looks synchronous.

```javascript
async function fetchData(url) {
  try {
    const response = await fetch(url);
    const data = await response.json();
    return data;
  } catch (err) {
    console.error("Error:", err);
  }
}
```

- **Generators**: A unique function form that can pause and resume execution, used in advanced async patterns or custom iterators.

9.2 Embracing Modern Frameworks and Build Tools

Frameworks like **React**, **Vue**, and **Angular** rely heavily on function usage—be it functional components, hooks, or watchers. Build tools (Webpack, Rollup, Vite) also optimize how your code is bundled and loaded, further blurring lines between front-end and back-end JavaScript usage.

9.3 Final Thoughts

JavaScript functions are the bedrock of any dynamic web experience. From straightforward utility functions to advanced patterns like closures, higher-order functions, asynchronous operations, and event handlers, they empower you to break down complex problems, handle user interactions fluidly, and orchestrate data flows in ways that remain clear and maintainable.

In this chapter, you dove into:

- **Defining and structuring functions** for reusability and clarity.

- **Event listeners** for making pages interactive based on user actions, from clicks to keyboard input.

- **A real-world "live search bar"** example showcasing how to combine user events with function logic for immediate, dynamic feedback.

- **Advanced techniques** like closures, memoization, and best practices in error handling, debugging, and security.

By mastering these concepts, you're well on your way to building powerful, smart web applications that delight your users. JavaScript's flexibility can be both an asset and a challenge, but a firm grasp of functions—and the patterns they unlock—puts you firmly in control of crafting responsive, efficient, and secure web experiences. Keep exploring, experiment with real-world projects, and embrace the ongoing evolution of the JavaScript ecosystem. Your functions will thank you—and so will your users.

Chapter 8: Form Handling in HTML: Collecting Data from Users

---

1. Introduction to Form Handling

In the world of web development, **forms** serve as the primary gateway for collecting user information—be it a simple contact form, a registration workflow, or a robust data entry interface. Forms allow users to communicate with your application by submitting data to the server, where it can be processed, validated, stored, and used for various purposes.

Form handling is not just about placing text fields and a "Submit" button on a page. It involves understanding **user experience (UX)**, **accessibility**, **security**, and **performance** considerations. The goal is to make data collection seamless and intuitive, ensuring that users can quickly and safely complete tasks.

In this chapter, we will explore how to craft effective, accessible, and secure forms in HTML, then validate them using **JavaScript**. We will also build a **real-world registration form** that highlights best practices for gathering user data.

2. The Fundamentals of HTML Forms

2.1 Why Forms Are Crucial for Web Applications

Whenever an application needs **user input**, forms typically come into play. They are the backbone for:

- **Account Creation**: Gathering usernames, emails, and passwords.

- **Search Bars**: Accepting search queries and filtering results.

- **Feedback/Contact**: Allowing users to share comments or ask questions.

- **E-Commerce**: Handling order placement, shipping information, and payment details.

Given their importance, designing forms that are intuitive and easy to fill out is vital to keeping users engaged and completing tasks.

2.2 Basic Form Structure

In HTML, every form resides within the <form> element:

```html
```

```
<form action="/submit" method="POST">
```

```
<label for="username">Username:</label>
<input type="text" id="username"
name="username">


<label for="password">Password:</label>
<input type="password" id="password"
name="password">


<button type="submit">Register</button>
</form>
```

Key attributes of the <form> tag:

- **action**: Specifies where form data is sent upon submission (e.g., a URL endpoint on your server).

- **method**: Dictates how data is sent—commonly GET or POST.

2.3 Common Input Types (Text, Email, Password, etc.)

HTML offers various input types that simplify both user input and validation:

1. **Text Fields**: <input type="text"> is the standard field for short textual input.

2. **Email Fields:** <input type="email"> can trigger automatic validation for email formats.

3. **Password Fields:** <input type="password"> masks characters for privacy.

4. **Number:** <input type="number"> restricts input to numeric values, sometimes with spinners for up/down increments.

5. **Checkbox:** <input type="checkbox"> toggles between two states (checked/unchecked).

6. **Radio Buttons:** <input type="radio"> for mutually exclusive choices.

7. **Select Menus** (<select>): Offer multiple or single selections from a dropdown.

8. **Textarea:** <textarea> for multi-line input.

Choosing the correct input type can drastically reduce the complexity of validation. For example, a <input type="email"> will not accept invalid addresses, providing a layer of built-in defense.

2.4 Labels and Accessibility Considerations

A **label** is crucial for screen readers and helps all users understand what information the form expects. The <label> element should either wrap the input or reference it through the for attribute:

html

```
<label for="email">Email:</label>
<input type="email" id="email" name="user_email" required>
```

This ensures assistive technologies read out the label when focusing on the corresponding input. Proper labeling also benefits sighted users by clearly matching input fields to their descriptions.

2.5 The Role of the name Attribute and Form Submission

When the form is submitted, the browser sends key-value pairs where **the key is the name attribute**, and **the value is what the user typed:**

html

```
<input type="text" name="username">
```

This might transform into username=john_doe when sent to the server. Without a name attribute, the data from that field will not be included in the submission payload.

---

3. Form Submission Mechanics

3.1 GET vs. POST Methods

- **GET**: Appends form data to the URL (e.g., example.com/search?query=term). This is convenient for bookmarkable or shareable URLs (like search queries) but not secure for sensitive data.

- **POST**: Sends the data in the body of the HTTP request, hiding it from casual onlookers. Usually preferred for handling user credentials, payments, or any data you wouldn't want in a URL.

3.2 Action URLs and How Data Travels to the Server

The **action** attribute in <form> indicates the server endpoint:

```html
<form action="/login" method="POST">
```

```
. . .
</form>
```

When the user submits, the browser compiles the form data, and if method="POST", it sends an HTTP POST request to /login, carrying the input data in its body.

3.3 Encoding Types (application/x-www-form-urlencoded, multipart/form-data)

By default, HTML forms use application/x-www-form-urlencoded encoding, suitable for text data. If you need to upload files, you must add enctype="multipart/form-data":

```html

<form action="/upload" method="POST"
enctype="multipart/form-data">
  <label for="photo">Choose a file:</label>
  <input type="file" id="photo" name="photo">
  <button type="submit">Upload</button>
</form>
```

3.4 Using target and Additional Form Attributes

- **target="_blank"**: Opens the response in a new tab/window.

- **novalidate**: Disables built-in HTML5 validation, giving you total control.

- **autocomplete="on|off"**: Suggests whether the browser should enable autofill.

---

4. Building Intuitive User Experiences

4.1 Logical Grouping with Fieldsets and Legends

When forms get more complex—like an address form combined with payment details—using <fieldset> can group related fields:

html

```
<fieldset>
  <legend>Shipping Address</legend>
  <label>Street:</label>
  <input type="text" name="street">
  ...
</fieldset>
```

The <legend> describes the grouping, aiding accessibility and clarity.

4.2 Placeholder Text and Inline Hints

<input placeholder="Enter your username"> is helpful, but avoid relying solely on placeholders for essential instructions. They disappear once the user starts typing, so combining placeholders with well-structured labels ensures clarity and accessibility.

4.3 Required Fields vs. Optional Fields

Marking a field as required communicates importance:

```html

<input type="text" name="first_name" required>
```

You can style [required] in CSS to highlight mandatory fields. However, also consider an explicit note like "required" or "optional" near each label for maximum clarity.

4.4 Designing for Mobile and Smaller Screens

Use **responsive design** techniques to ensure your form is easy to read on phones. For instance:

- **Large, Touch-Friendly Buttons**: Aim for a minimum tap target of around 40-48px in height.

- **Resizeable Text Fields**: Make sure input widths are set to 100% where possible.

- **Simplified Layout**: Only ask for essential data. Mobile users may abandon forms if they're too lengthy.

5. Advanced HTML5 Form Features

5.1 Built-in Validation Attributes (required, pattern, etc.)

Modern HTML can validate many inputs before you even involve JavaScript:

- **required**: Blocks submission unless the field is filled in.

- **pattern="[A-Za-z0-9_]{5,12}"**: Enforces a regular expression check (e.g., username must be 5-12 alphanumeric characters).

- **type="email"**: Ensures the input matches an email format.

- **min, max, step**: For numeric fields, limiting acceptable ranges or increments.

5.2 New Input Types (date, time, range, color, etc.)

HTML5 introduced a variety of new input types:

- **<input type="date">**: Provides a calendar UI in many browsers.

- **<input type="time">**: Lets users select time using a dropdown or clock.

- **\<input type="range"\>**: A slider for picking numeric values.

- **\<input type="color"\>**: Opens a color picker in some browsers.

While not all browsers support every feature, they can gracefully degrade. If a browser doesn't support type="date", it typically treats it like a plain text field.

5.3 Autofocus, Autocomplete, and Other Helpers

- **autofocus**: The field receives focus automatically when the page loads.

- **autocomplete="off"**: Disables browser autofill suggestions.

- **autocomplete="new-password"**: Instructs the browser to suggest a new password, beneficial in signup forms.

Used correctly, these helpers speed up data entry and reduce user friction.

---

6. Validating User Input with JavaScript

6.1 When and Why to Validate Client-Side

Client-side validation provides immediate feedback, improving user experience by catching mistakes like an empty email field before the form is submitted. This can reduce server load because fewer invalid submissions arrive at the back end.

However, **client-side validation** shouldn't replace **server-side validation**—users can disable JavaScript, or malicious actors could craft requests that bypass your form entirely.

6.2 Key Validation Patterns (Regex, Conditional Checks, etc.)

JavaScript offers multiple ways to validate data:

1. **Regular Expressions (Regex)**: Ideal for checking format constraints (email patterns, phone numbers, alphanumeric rules, etc.).

2. **Conditional Checks**: E.g., ensuring a "confirm password" field matches the main password.

3. **List or Range Checks**: If a user must select from a set of valid options, ensure they do so.

6.3 Real-Time Feedback vs. On-Submit Validation

- **Real-Time/On-Blur Validation**: Provide immediate alerts, highlighting the specific fields that fail. This approach guides users as they fill out the form, but can be distracting if overused.

- **On-Submit Validation**: Waits until the user clicks "Submit" or presses Enter. This is simpler, but mistakes might accumulate, leading to a bigger fix at the end.

Finding a balance is key. Some forms do both: real-time checks for critical fields (like email addresses or password strength) and final checks when the form is submitted.

6.4 Handling Edge Cases and Security Concerns

From a security standpoint, it's vital to remember that **JavaScript validation can be bypassed** by turning off JavaScript or by sending data through other tools. Also consider:

- **Hidden Fields**: Malicious users might tweak hidden input values.

- **Spam/Abuse**: Implement measures like **CAPTCHA** or honeypot fields for forms likely to attract bots.

Always re-validate data on the server side.

7. Real-World Example: Building a Registration Form

7.1 Project Overview and Goals

Let's imagine creating a **user registration** page for a new web application. We want users to provide:

- **Username**: Must be alphanumeric, 5-12 characters.

- **Email**: Must follow a valid email format.

- **Password**: At least 8 characters, recommended complexity.

- **Confirm Password**: Must match the Password field.

We'll incorporate both **HTML5 validations** and **custom JavaScript** to demonstrate best practices.

7.2 HTML Structure for Registration

Create a file named register.html:

html

```
<!DOCTYPE html>
<html lang="en">
<head>
  <meta charset="UTF-8">
  <title>User Registration</title>
  <link rel="stylesheet" href="styles.css">
</head>
<body>
  <h1>Register for Our Application</h1>
  <form id="registrationForm">
    <label for="username">Username (5-12 chars,
alphanumeric):</label>
    <input
      type="text"
      id="username"
      name="username"
      pattern="[A-Za-z0-9_]{5,12}"
      required
```

```
  >

  <label for="email">Email:</label>
  <input
    type="email"
    id="email"
    name="email"
    required
  >

  <label for="password">Password (min 8
chars):</label>
  <input
    type="password"
    id="password"
    name="password"
    minlength="8"
    required
  >

  <label for="confirmPassword">Confirm
Password:</label>
  <input
    type="password"
    id="confirmPassword"
    name="confirmPassword"
```

```
  minlength="8"
  required
>


<button type="submit">Create Account</button>
</form>


<script src="app.js"></script>
</body>
</html>
```

7.3 Applying Basic CSS for Clarity

In styles.css:

css

```css
body {
  font-family: Arial, sans-serif;
  margin: 20px auto;
  max-width: 400px;
}


h1 {
  text-align: center;
}


form {
```

```
  display: flex;
  flex-direction: column;
}


label {
  margin-top: 15px;
}


input {
  padding: 8px;
  font-size: 1em;
  margin-top: 5px;
}


button {
  margin-top: 20px;
  padding: 10px;
  cursor: pointer;
}
```

This ensures the form looks neat. Inputs stack vertically, providing a straightforward, mobile-friendly layout.

7.4 Implementing Client-Side Validation with JavaScript

Now, create app.js to handle custom checks:

```javascript
document.addEventListener("DOMContentLoaded", ()
=> {
  const form =
document.getElementById("registrationForm");
  const usernameInput =
document.getElementById("username");
  const emailInput =
document.getElementById("email");
  const passwordInput =
document.getElementById("password");
  const confirmPasswordInput =
document.getElementById("confirmPassword");

  form.addEventListener("submit", (event) => {
    // Check if password fields match
    if (passwordInput.value !==
confirmPasswordInput.value) {
      event.preventDefault();
      alert("Passwords do not match. Please re-
enter.");
      return;
    }

    // Optional: Additional checks or logging
```

```
    console.log("All client-side validations
passed!");
    // If you want to actually see server
behavior, you'd remove event.preventDefault()
    // and ensure there's a real action URL or
handling mechanism in place.
  });
});
```

Walkthrough:

1. **DOMContentLoaded** ensures the script runs only after the DOM is fully loaded.

2. We select all relevant inputs using getElementById.

3. **On submit** (form.addEventListener("submit", …)), we check if the two password fields match. If not, we preventDefault() to stop form submission and show an alert.

4. If everything is good, we log to the console and allow the form to submit.

7.5 Progressive Enhancement and Graceful Degradation

- If **JavaScript is disabled**, HTML5 validation still ensures mandatory fields and patterns. But the "password match" check would fail silently. On the back end, we must re-check.

- If the **browser** doesn't support pattern checks, it'll default to a regular text field, so the user can type anything—but again, server-side rules must ensure correctness.

This approach ensures that advanced features enhance user experience without making the form unusable in older environments.

---

8. Enhancing Accessibility and UX

8.1 Semantic Markup and Assistive Technologies

Using <label> with for ensures screen readers announce the correct label for each field. A robust approach might also incorporate **aria-describedby** to point to help text or error messages, providing additional context.

8.2 Using ARIA Attributes Appropriately

For forms that dynamically display or hide fields, consider **ARIA attributes** such as aria-expanded to indicate if a collapsible section is open. This can help screen readers interpret the UI changes.

8.3 Error Messaging Best Practices

When forms fail, guiding the user is crucial. Instead of a single alert, you can display inline errors near each problematic field:

```html
html
```

```html
<div id="usernameError" class="error-message"
aria-live="polite"></div>
```

When an error occurs, populate that div with the relevant message. Setting aria-live="polite" ensures screen readers automatically announce new error text.

---

9. Server-Side Considerations

9.1 Why Server-Side Validation Is Also Critical

No matter how robust your client-side checks, you cannot trust data until it's validated on the server. A malicious user can skip or disable client-side scripts, sending raw requests that don't match your expected format.

9.2 Session Handling and Security

After successful form submission, you typically create a **session** for the user—especially for registrations or logins. This session might set a **cookie** or token to identify the user in subsequent requests. Carefully handle tokens and session IDs to prevent **session hijacking**.

9.3 Storing User Data and Database Integration (Brief Overview)

Upon receiving form data, the server code might:

1. **Validate** the data again.

2. **Hash and salt** user passwords using a secure algorithm like bcrypt.

3. **Insert** the data into a database table.

4. **Generate** a response, possibly redirecting to a "success" page.

10. Performance, Security, and Testing

10.1 Minimizing Form Load Times

Large forms with many scripts or heavy libraries can slow page loads. Some ways to optimize:

- **Load scripts asynchronously** or at the page bottom.

- **Compress** and **minify** CSS/JS.

- **Use fewer images**, or lazy-load them if not immediately visible.

10.2 Addressing Common Security Concerns (XSS, CSRF)

- **Cross-Site Scripting (XSS)**: If your form data is displayed back to the user, sanitize or encode special characters to prevent script injection.

- **Cross-Site Request Forgery (CSRF)**: Use tokens to ensure that a form submission came from your site, not a malicious third-party page.

10.3 Tools and Techniques for Automated Testing

Jest, **Mocha**, or **Cypress** can automate form testing, verifying that fields display correctly, validation triggers as expected, and data flows to your server endpoints. End-to-end tests with tools like **Puppeteer** or **Playwright** can simulate real user interactions.

---

11. Conclusion

Form handling is a **keystone** skill in front-end and full-stack web development. From placing basic fields and labels to advanced HTML5 attributes, from simple JavaScript checks to robust server-side validation, you have a wealth of tools to collect data efficiently and securely. When done well, forms provide a smooth, intuitive user experience that fosters trust and user satisfaction.

Key takeaways from this chapter include:

1. **HTML Fundamentals**: Use <form> elements, correct method attributes, and well-labeled inputs for clarity and accessibility.

2. **Validation**: Leverage HTML5 built-in validations and enhance with **JavaScript** to provide immediate feedback—without neglecting **server-side** checks.

3. **Real-World Registration Example**: A blueprint for typical user sign-up forms, integrating pattern matching, password confirmation, and best practices for layout and labeling.

4. **Accessibility and Security**: You must serve all users, including those with assistive technologies, and protect the integrity of data with server-side checks and security measures like CSRF tokens.

Armed with these principles, you can confidently build web forms that are both user-friendly and robust. As you progress, you'll refine your approach to form design, ensuring every detail—from placeholder usage to error messaging—reflects a seamless, professional experience.

Chapter 9: CSS Flexbox and Grid: Advanced Layout Techniques

---

1. Introduction to Modern CSS Layouts

For years, web designers relied on **floats, tables,** or even **absolute positioning** hacks to arrange elements on a webpage. These techniques often led to complex, fragile layouts that were time-consuming to maintain. With the advent of **CSS Flexbox** and **CSS Grid**, modern web development has taken a quantum leap, providing powerful, intuitive ways to create sophisticated and responsive layouts.

- **Flexbox** shines for **one-dimensional** layouts—arranging elements in a row or a column while easily controlling spacing, alignment, and reordering.

- **Grid** excels in **two-dimensional** layouts—defining rows and columns simultaneously, giving you unprecedented control over complex, magazine-style or dashboard-like designs.

This chapter delves into how each method works, clarifies when to choose one over the other, and presents a real-world example of creating a **modern, responsive blog layout** that leverages both Flexbox and Grid. By the end, you'll have a comprehensive understanding of these layout techniques, empowering you to build sophisticated, user-friendly interfaces that adapt gracefully to various screen sizes.

---

2. The Power of Flexbox

2.1. Flex Containers and Flex Items

Flexbox (Flexible Box Layout) is designed to distribute space along a single axis, either horizontally or vertically. When you declare a container as a **flex container**, all its direct children become **flex**

items, gaining special properties that let you manipulate their size and spacing with ease.

css

```
.container {
  display: flex; /* This makes .container a flex
container */
}
```

Any <div>, <section>, or other element inside .container is treated as a flex item. The default direction is **row**, meaning items line up horizontally.

2.2. Core Flexbox Properties

Flexbox unlocks a suite of specialized properties that let you define how items stretch, shrink, or align within their container:

1. **flex-direction**: Determines the main axis (row, row-reverse, column, column-reverse).

2. **justify-content**: Controls how items are spaced along the main axis (flex-start, flex-end, center, space-between, space-around, space-evenly).

3. **align-items**: Dictates how items align along the cross axis (stretch, flex-start, flex-end, center, baseline).

4. **flex-wrap**: Tells the container whether items should wrap onto new lines if they overflow.

5. **align-content**: Adjusts spacing along the cross axis when there's room for multiple rows or columns of flex items.

A common pattern is a row of navigation links:

css

```css
.nav {
  display: flex;
  justify-content: space-between;
  align-items: center;
  background-color: #333;
}
.nav a {
  color: #fff;
  margin: 0 15px;
  text-decoration: none;
}
```

Here, justify-content: space-between pushes one item to the extreme left, another to the extreme right, with remaining items distributed in between.

2.3. Realigning and Ordering Elements

Flexbox also lets you reorder elements visually without changing the HTML structure. The **order** property determines how items are placed in the layout, where a smaller order value appears first. This feature is useful for responsive designs where you might want a sidebar to appear below the main content on mobile, but to the left or right on desktop, all without duplicating markup.

2.4. Advanced Flexbox Techniques

2.4.1. Flex-Wrapping for Responsive Rows

By default, flex items try to fit into a single row (or column). When content can't shrink further, it overflows. flex-wrap solves this problem:

css

```
.gallery {
  display: flex;
  flex-wrap: wrap;
}
```

Now items automatically wrap onto new lines instead of breaking the layout.

2.4.2. Distributing Space with flex Shorthand

flex is a powerful shorthand that controls how an item grows or shrinks relative to its siblings. It can accept up to three values: flex-grow, flex-shrink, and flex-basis:

css

```css
.item {
  flex: 1 1 200px; /* Grows if there's space,
shrinks if needed, starts at 200px width */
}
```

- 1 (flex-grow) means the item can expand to fill space relative to others.

- 1 (flex-shrink) means the item can also shrink if needed.

- 200px (flex-basis) sets the starting size.

2.4.3. Vertical Centering Without Hassle

One of the most-touted benefits of Flexbox is its simplicity for **vertical centering**:

css

```css
.centered-container {
  display: flex;
  justify-content: center; /* horizontally */
```

```
  align-items: center; /* vertically */
  height: 100vh;
}
```

The content inside .centered-container is perfectly centered both horizontally and vertically—something that used to be quite tricky with older layout methods.

---

3. Understanding CSS Grid

3.1. Grid Containers and Grid Items

While Flexbox arranges items along one axis at a time, **CSS Grid** is built for **two-dimensional** layouts. This is ideal for complex websites with rows and columns that must align in a more structured manner.

css

```
.grid-container {
  display: grid; /* Declares .grid-container as a
grid container */
}
```

Immediately, child elements become **grid items**, each occupying the cells defined by your grid tracks.

3.2. Defining Tracks: grid-template-columns and grid-template-rows

To create columns and rows, use grid-template-columns and grid-template-rows. For example:

css

```css
.grid-container {
  display: grid;
  grid-template-columns: 200px 1fr 1fr;
  grid-template-rows: auto auto;
  gap: 20px; /* Gap between cells */
}
```

- **200px 1fr 1fr** sets the first column to a fixed width of 200px, and the next two columns to flexible fractions of the remaining space.

- **auto auto** for rows means they will size themselves based on content, with each row occupying as much space as needed.

- **gap: 20px** (or the older grid-gap) inserts spacing between columns and rows without extra margin or padding hacks.

3.3. Grid Lines, Areas, and the Power of Named Lines

One of Grid's superpowers is the ability to place items on specific rows and columns by referencing **grid lines**:

css

```
.item1 {
  grid-column: 1 / 2; /* from column line 1 to
column line 2 */
  grid-row: 1 / 3;    /* from row line 1 to row
line 3 */
}
```

Alternatively, you can name areas in your container and place items accordingly. For example:

css

```
.grid-container {
  display: grid;
  grid-template-areas:
    "header header header"
    "sidebar content content"
    "footer footer footer";
  grid-template-columns: 200px 1fr 1fr;
  grid-template-rows: auto 1fr auto;
```

```
}

.header {
  grid-area: header;
}
.sidebar {
  grid-area: sidebar;
}
.content {
  grid-area: content;
}
.footer {
  grid-area: footer;
}
```

This approach is especially intuitive when working with complex designs or prototyping layouts before the content is fully determined.

3.4. Implicit vs. Explicit Grids

- **Explicit Grid**: Defined using grid-template-* properties. This is the layout you explicitly create.

- **Implicit Grid**: If you place an item in a row/column outside your defined area, Grid automatically creates new rows or columns to accommodate it. This is the "implicit grid."

For large dynamic content, you may rely on the implicit grid to handle overflow gracefully. But keep in mind that you can style these implicit tracks using grid-auto-rows or grid-auto-columns.

3.5. Advanced Grid Features (auto-fit, auto-fill, minmax, etc.)

CSS Grid includes advanced features that automate layout decisions:

1. **auto-fit / auto-fill**: Repeats columns or rows to fill available space, perfect for responsive image galleries.

2. **minmax(min, max)**: Lets each track dynamically size between a minimum and maximum value:

css

```
grid-template-columns: repeat(auto-fill,
minmax(200px, 1fr));
```

Each column is at least 200px wide, but can stretch up to 1fr if space allows.

3. **fr Unit**: A fraction unit that represents a portion of the leftover space in the grid container, simplifying fluid layouts without manually using percentages or calc.

4. When to Use Flexbox vs. Grid

4.1. Deciding Factors in Design Patterns

- **Flexbox:** Best for simpler, one-dimensional layouts: navbars, menus, horizontal or vertical alignment of items, or small card layouts that don't require intricate row/column spanning.

- **Grid:** Ideal for multi-dimensional designs: magazine-like layouts, dashboard UIs, or any layout that needs precise row and column control.

4.2. Combining Both for Complex Layouts

Modern UIs often blend **Grid** for the overarching two-dimensional structure (header, sidebar, content, footer) and **Flexbox** for fine-tuning items within each section (like horizontally distributing nav links or vertically centering a hero section).

4.3. Performance and Browser Support Considerations

- **Flexbox** is well-supported across all major browsers, including older versions if you use vendor prefixes.

- **Grid** is fully supported in modern browsers (Chrome, Firefox, Safari, Edge), but older IE versions do not natively support the official spec. Where older support is needed, you might rely on polyfills or fallbacks.

- Performance-wise, both Flexbox and Grid are hardware-accelerated in most modern browsers, and you rarely see significant performance differences for typical page layouts.

---

5. Real-World Example: Creating a Modern, Responsive Blog Layout

5.1. Project Overview and Goals

Imagine we're building a **tech blog** with the following sections:

1. A **header** containing the site logo, name, and main navigation.

2. A **main content area** featuring a list of blog posts (each as a card).

3. A **sidebar** that includes an "About Me" blurb, a list of categories, and social media links.

4. A **footer** with copyright and contact info.

We want a layout that scales from **mobile** (single-column) to **desktop** (a broader, two-column display with a clearly defined sidebar).

5.2. Building the Structure with HTML

Below is a simplified version of index.html:

```html
html
```

```html
<!DOCTYPE html>
<html lang="en">
<head>
  <meta charset="UTF-8">
  <title>TechPro Blog</title>
  <link rel="stylesheet" href="styles.css">
```

```html
</head>
<body>
  <header class="site-header">
    <div class="logo">TechPro</div>
    <nav class="main-nav">
      <ul>
        <li><a href="#">Home</a></li>
        <li><a href="#">Articles</a></li>
        <li><a href="#">Tutorials</a></li>
        <li><a href="#">Contact</a></li>
      </ul>
    </nav>
  </header>

  <div class="container">
    <main class="content-area">
      <article class="post">
        <h2 class="post-title">Understanding CSS Grid</h2>
        <p class="post-excerpt">Grid is a game-changer for modern layouts...</p>
        <a href="#" class="read-more">Read More</a>
      </article>
      <article class="post">
```

```
    <h2 class="post-title">Flexbox: A
Comprehensive Guide</h2>
    <p class="post-excerpt">Learn how to
align, distribute space, and reorder
elements...</p>
    <a href="#" class="read-more">Read
More</a>
  </article>
  <!-- Add more posts as needed -->
</main>


<aside class="sidebar">
  <section class="about-me">
    <h3>About Me</h3>
    <p>Hi, I'm Alex. Passionate about front-
end engineering and design...</p>
  </section>
  <section class="categories">
    <h3>Categories</h3>
    <ul>
      <li><a href="#">CSS</a></li>
      <li><a href="#">JavaScript</a></li>
      <li><a href="#">HTML</a></li>
      <li><a href="#">React</a></li>
    </ul>
  </section>
```

```html
<section class="social-links">
  <h3>Follow Me</h3>
  <ul>
    <li><a href="#">Twitter</a></li>
    <li><a href="#">GitHub</a></li>
    <li><a href="#">LinkedIn</a></li>
  </ul>
</section>
</aside>
</div>

<footer class="site-footer">
  <p>&copy; 2025 TechPro Blog</p>
</footer>
</body>
</html>
```

5.3. Applying Flexbox for the Header and Navigation

In styles.css, we'll handle the header with **Flexbox** to align the logo and navigation:

css

```css
body {
  margin: 0;
```

```css
  font-family: Arial, sans-serif;
  color: #333;
}


.site-header {
  display: flex;
  align-items: center;
  justify-content: space-between;
  background-color: #222;
  padding: 10px 20px;
}


.logo {
  font-size: 1.5em;
  color: #fff;
}


.main-nav ul {
  display: flex;
  list-style-type: none;
  margin: 0;
  padding: 0;
}


.main-nav li a {
  color: #fff;
```

```
text-decoration: none;
margin: 0 10px;
}
```

- **display: flex** on .site-header places the .logo and .main-nav on the same row.

- **justify-content: space-between** ensures the logo is left-aligned and navigation is right-aligned.

- The nav links are also flex items, spaced horizontally via margin.

5.4. Using Grid for the Main Content and Sidebar

Now, we'll declare a **Grid** layout for the .container that holds .content-area (main blog posts) and .sidebar:

css

```
.container {
  display: grid;
  grid-template-columns: 1fr;
  gap: 20px;
  padding: 20px;
}

/* On larger screens, switch to two columns */
@media (min-width: 768px) {
```

```css
.container {
  grid-template-columns: 3fr 1fr;
}
}


.content-area {
  background-color: #f9f9f9;
  padding: 20px;
}


.sidebar {
  background-color: #f0f0f0;
  padding: 20px;
}
```

- By default (on mobile or narrower screens), we have a single-column layout: **grid-template-columns: 1fr;**.

- When the viewport is at least 768px, we switch to **two columns**: 3fr for the main content and 1fr for the sidebar.

- gap: 20px; sets a nice spacing between columns (and potential rows, if any item extends in height or wraps).

5.5. Responsiveness and Media Queries

We already used a media query for the container. Let's refine it further:

css

```css
@media (max-width: 767px) {
  .site-header {
    flex-direction: column;
    align-items: flex-start;
  }
  .main-nav ul {
    flex-direction: column;
  }
  .main-nav li a {
    margin: 5px 0;
  }
}
```

- On small screens (max-width: 767px), the header stacks vertically.

- Navigation links become a vertical list, easier to tap with a thumb.

5.6. Testing and Refining the Layout

1. **Check Mobile**: On a phone or emulator, the blog should display the header (logo above nav), followed by single-column main content, then the sidebar below it.

2. **Check Tablet:** On a tablet or mid-sized screen, .container splits into two columns. The sidebar sits on the right.

3. **Check Desktop:** The layout should remain consistent, with extra space for the .content-area. The sidebar remains at a fixed fraction of the container.

If the posts list is too wide or you need additional columns for the content area, consider applying a sub-grid or using multiple columns inside .content-area with either Flexbox or Grid.

---

6. Advanced Tips, Tricks, and Troubleshooting

6.1. Dealing with Overflow and Scrollable Containers

Sometimes you might want a **scrollable sidebar** while keeping the main content fixed:

css

```
.sidebar {
  max-height: 80vh;
```

```
  overflow-y: auto; /* Let it scroll if content
exceeds 80% of the viewport */
}
```

Use overflow-y: auto with caution to avoid creating unintuitive scrolling experiences.

6.2. Nesting Flex and Grid Containers

Nesting is common. For instance, your .content-area can be declared as a **grid** if you want to show a masonry-like arrangement of blog cards. Inside those cards, you might use **flex** to align an icon and text horizontally. This layered approach is a hallmark of modern CSS layouts.

6.3. Creating Fluid, Complex Layouts with fr Units

Grid's fr units are a game-changer:

css

```
.grid-gallery {
  display: grid;
  grid-template-columns: repeat(auto-fit,
minmax(200px, 1fr));
  gap: 10px;
}
```

As the container shrinks, columns wrap automatically, ensuring each column remains at least 200px. On larger viewports, more columns appear. This fluid approach is perfect for image galleries, product listings, or portfolio grids.

6.4. Handling Older Browser Support

- **Autoprefixer:** Tools like Autoprefixer in your build pipeline ensure older browsers see appropriate vendor prefixes.

- **Graceful Degradation:** Provide a simpler layout for browsers that lack modern CSS features.

- **Feature Queries:** Use @supports (display: grid) to apply grid styles only if the user's browser supports them, ensuring fallback for others.

---

7. Accessibility and SEO Considerations for Layout

7.1. Semantic Markup and Landmarks

Even with powerful layout systems like Flexbox and Grid, don't neglect **HTML5 landmarks**—<header>, <nav>, <main>, <aside>, and <footer>. They inform both assistive technologies and search engines about your page structure.

7.2. Keyboard Navigation and Focus Order

CSS alone doesn't affect the **tab** order of elements. The DOM order remains crucial for keyboard users. If you reorder content visually via order in Flexbox or grid placement, ensure the logical reading order still makes sense.

7.3. Maintaining Logical Reading Order

A complex layout shouldn't hamper usability. Resist the temptation to reorder items so drastically that visually they appear in a different sequence than the DOM order. Screen reader users might otherwise be confused by mismatched reading flows.

---

8. Performance Optimization for Layouts

8.1. Minimizing Reflows

Every time the browser recalculates positions (a **reflow**), it can be costly for performance. Overusing properties that frequently shift layout—like changing grid-template-rows or toggling display—can cause noticeable lag. If you animate layout changes, prefer transforming individual elements with transform: translate() or opacity, which typically doesn't trigger reflow.

8.2. Using GPU Acceleration for Animations

By applying will-change: transform; or translateZ(0) to elements, you can nudge some browsers to use the GPU for smoother animations. However, overusing will-change can lead to memory bloat, so apply it judiciously.

8.3. Efficient Rendering with Minimal Layout Thrashing

When making multiple changes to the DOM—especially in JavaScript—batch them together. For instance, read layout properties (like offsetWidth) or CSS values in a separate batch from writing changes to the DOM (like style.left = "100px"). Interleaving too many reads and writes can cause layout thrashing and degrade performance.

9. Conclusion

CSS **Flexbox** and **Grid** have revolutionized the way we approach web layouts, moving us beyond the cumbersome hacks of floats and positioning. By combining:

- **Flexbox** for one-dimensional tasks (navbars, alignment, reorder)

- **Grid** for two-dimensional tasks (magazine-style layouts, major site sections)

...you can craft layouts that are both visually impressive and maintainable. The **real-world blog example** demonstrates how these tools work hand in hand to create a responsive, modern site that seamlessly scales from mobile to desktop.

Key takeaways:

1. **Choose the Right Tool**: Use Flexbox when you need to line up items on a single axis or control distribution. Use Grid when you want more advanced two-dimensional control.

2. **Embrace Responsiveness**: Media queries combined with fluid units (fr, minmax(), etc.) allow your layouts to adapt gracefully across devices.

3. **Balance Visual Reordering with Accessibility**: Keep in mind the DOM order for screen readers and keyboard navigation.

4. **Refine Performance**: Avoid frequent reflows; group layout reads/writes to ensure smooth user interactions.

5. **Test Across Devices and Browsers**: Leverage DevTools, emulators, and real devices to confirm your design holds up.

By mastering these advanced **CSS** layout techniques, you'll build experiences that impress end users, satisfy design demands, and stand the test of time. The synergy between Flexbox and Grid is a testament to how far **CSS** has evolved, empowering developers to deliver websites that are both elegant and efficient without resorting to clunky workarounds. Lean into these standards, and let your creativity shine in next-level layouts that engage users on every screen size.

Chapter 10: AJAX and Fetch API: Making Your Web Apps Dynamic

---

1. Introduction to Dynamic Web Applications

For much of the early web, pages were largely static; when users clicked a link or submitted a form, the browser would **reload** the entire page to display updated content. This created clunky transitions and poor user experiences—an era where each page load felt like hitting the "reset button" on the browser. However, with the rise of **AJAX** (Asynchronous JavaScript and XML) and subsequent developments like the **Fetch API**, front-end developers gained the ability to seamlessly fetch and update data in the background. No longer was a full-page reload necessary for every update. Instead, data can be requested from a server, processed, and **dynamically injected** into the existing page without interrupting the user flow.

Today, asynchronous data fetching underpins nearly all modern websites and web apps, from email clients that load new messages as they arrive, to interactive dashboards that refresh live metrics, to social media feeds that keep you updated without reloading. In this chapter, we'll explore how AJAX laid the foundation for dynamic web interactions and then dive into the **Fetch API**, the modern, promise-based approach to performing asynchronous requests. We'll build a **real-time weather application** that fetches data from a public **API** and updates the interface without ever forcing the user to reload. By the end, you'll be well-equipped to incorporate asynchronous features into any web application, delivering smooth, responsive user experiences.

---

2. What is AJAX?

2.1. The Origin of AJAX

The term **AJAX** was coined by Jesse James Garrett in 2005, though the underlying technologies existed beforehand. AJAX stands for **A**synchronous **J**ava**S**cript **a**nd **X**ML, but ironically XML is rarely used anymore—**JSON** (JavaScript Object Notation) has largely replaced it due to its lighter weight and simpler parsing in JavaScript. The fundamental idea behind AJAX was: "Why reload the entire page if you only need to change part of it?"

Key pieces of the AJAX puzzle historically included:

1. **XMLHttpRequest (XHR)**: A JavaScript API that allowed sending HTTP requests and receiving responses asynchronously.

2. **JavaScript + DOM**: The script that updates the Document Object Model to reflect new data, effectively changing only parts of the webpage.

3. **Data Format**: Initially XML, but over time JSON became the standard because it's simpler to use with JavaScript.

2.2. How AJAX Changed the Web

Before AJAX, web pages acted like discrete documents—you clicked a link or submitted a form, and the server sent back a new page. This hampered the creation of fluid, app-like experiences. AJAX allowed websites to behave more like **desktop applications** by updating parts of the interface instantly, based on user interactions or background events.

Some hallmark examples of AJAX-driven innovation include:

- **Gmail**: One of the first major webmail services to load new emails in the background.

- **Google Maps**: Seamlessly retrieving map tiles as you panned or zoomed.

- **Social Media Feeds**: Live updates that appear the moment someone posts or comments.

2.3. The Role of XMLHttpRequest (XHR)

XMLHttpRequest, introduced by Microsoft for Outlook Web Access in Internet Explorer 5, became the de facto engine behind AJAX in its early days. It allowed developers to do things like:

javascript

```
const xhr = new XMLHttpRequest();
xhr.open("GET", "https://api.example.com/data",
true);
xhr.onreadystatechange = function() {
  if (xhr.readyState === 4 && xhr.status === 200)
{
    console.log("Response:", xhr.responseText);
  }
};
xhr.send();
```

Although revolutionary at the time, the **XHR** interface can be verbose and tricky, with multiple readyStates to check, plus limited error-handling patterns. As the web evolved, developers looked for more streamlined ways to handle asynchronous requests—which led, in part, to the design of **the Fetch API**.

3. Core AJAX Concepts and Workflows

3.1. Asynchronous vs. Synchronous Operations

In a **synchronous** workflow, each operation blocks the execution thread until it completes. This means if you make a request to the server and wait for the response, the browser can't process user input during that period, leading to a "frozen" page. AJAX introduced an **asynchronous** model, where JavaScript can initiate a request and then move on to other tasks. When the server response returns, a callback handles the data, updating the UI with minimal disruption.

3.2. JSON, XML, and Other Data Formats

While the "X" in "AJAX" originally stood for XML, many modern apps rely on **JSON**. Its syntax mirrors JavaScript objects:

```json
json

{
  "weather": "Sunny",
  "temperature": 25
}
```

JavaScript can parse this directly with JSON.parse(...), making it easy to incorporate into front-end code. However, XML still appears in legacy systems or specialized cases. Some APIs even return CSV or custom data structures. The principles remain the same: you fetch the data asynchronously, parse it, and update the page.

3.3. Handling Responses and Errors

Effective AJAX calls handle both **success** and **failure** gracefully. When the server responds with a **2xx** (e.g., **200 OK**) status, you parse the data and update the UI. If the server returns a **4xx** (client error) or **5xx** (server error) code, or if the network is unavailable, your code should display an error message. This robust approach ensures a stable user experience even in non-ideal conditions, like intermittent connections or invalid inputs.

3.4. Common Use Cases for AJAX

- **Form Submissions**: Sending data without leaving the page, providing instant feedback or partial updates.

- **Live Searching**: Querying a database or service as the user types, delivering autocomplete suggestions.

- **Endless Scrolling**: Loading new content as the user nears the bottom of a page (typical in social feeds).

- **Real-Time Dashboards**: Updating charts or metrics periodically, often using setInterval or websockets.

---

4. From XHR to Fetch: The Evolution of Asynchronous Calls

4.1. Limitations of XMLHttpRequest

Despite its significance, XMLHttpRequest can feel cumbersome:

- **Event Handling**: Checking readyState and status can be verbose.

- **Callbacks**: Tends to lead to callback-heavy code.

- **No Streams**: XHR doesn't natively support streaming the response in smaller chunks.

- **Verbose Syntax**: You must manually configure each step (open, onreadystatechange, etc.).

4.2. Introducing the Fetch API

The **Fetch API** was introduced to simplify these workflows. It's modern, promise-based, and more versatile. Here's a simple example:

javascript

```
fetch("https://api.example.com/data")
  .then(response => {
    if (!response.ok) {
      throw new Error(`Network error:
${response.status}`);
    }
    return response.json();
  })
  .then(data => {
    console.log("Received data:", data);
  })
  .catch(err => {
    console.error("Fetch failed:", err);
  });
```

In a single chain, we handle **the request, response parsing, error checking,** and **error handling.** The promises approach also integrates cleanly with **async/await** syntax.

4.3. Comparing XHR and Fetch at a Glance

Feature	XHR	Fetch
Syntax	Callback / Event-based	Promise-based

Error Handling	Must handle manually	Automatic with throw on bad status (if you wish)
Streaming	Limited support	ReadableStream can be used (in modern browsers)
Simplicity	More verbose	Concise, modern
Browser Support	Very old versions of IE	Widely supported, IE requires polyfill

While you can still use XMLHttpRequest for certain legacy scenarios, **Fetch** is the recommended approach for building modern web apps.

---

5. Using Fetch API: How to Fetch Data from Servers without Reloading the Page

5.1. Basic Syntax of Fetch

The basic **Fetch** call is:

```javascript
fetch("url")
  .then(response => {
    // handle the response
```

```
})
.catch(error => {
  // handle network errors
});
```

fetch always returns a **promise**, which resolves to a **Response** object. You can then parse that response (as text, JSON, blob, etc.).

5.2. Handling Promises and Response Objects

A standard pattern involves:

1. **Check if response.ok**: If the status is between 200 and 299.

2. **Parse the Body**: Typically using response.json() or response.text().

3. **Handle the Parsed Data**: Update the DOM accordingly.

5.3. Parsing JSON Data

JSON is ubiquitous in modern APIs. After you get the **Response** object:

```javascript

fetch("https://api.example.com/items")
  .then(response => {
    if (!response.ok) {
```

```javascript
      throw new Error(`Server returned status:
${response.status}`);
    }
    return response.json(); // parse as JSON
  })
  .then(jsonData => {
    console.log("Parsed JSON:", jsonData);
  })
  .catch(err => {
    console.error("Error in fetch call:", err);
  });
```

5.4. POST Requests with Fetch

Sending data to the server (e.g., form submissions) is easy with **POST**:

javascript

```javascript
fetch("https://api.example.com/users", {
  method: "POST",
  headers: { "Content-Type": "application/json" },
  body: JSON.stringify({ username: "JohnDoe",
email: "john@example.com" })
})
  .then(response => {
    if (!response.ok) {
```

```
    throw new Error("Network response was not
ok");
    }
    return response.json();
  })
  .then(data => {
    console.log("User created:", data);
  })
  .catch(err => console.error("Request failed:",
err));
```

Here, we specify the **method**, relevant **headers**, and include the request **body** (converted to a JSON string).

5.5. Error Handling and Network Failures

Unlike XHR, the **Fetch** call only rejects the promise on **network failure**, not for HTTP errors (4xx or 5xx). That's why checking response.ok is crucial. This approach separates "bad server status" from actual network errors like offline or DNS issues.

6. Real-World Example: Creating a Real-Time Weather App

Let's cement these concepts by building a **live weather dashboard**. We'll fetch data from an external weather API, parse the response, and dynamically update the page.

6.1. Overview of the Weather App

Features:

1. **Search** by city name.

2. **Display** current temperature, weather conditions, and a relevant icon.

3. **Update** the page without reloading.

Tech:

- **HTML/CSS** for the interface.

- **JavaScript** (Fetch) for data retrieval.

- A free weather API (e.g., OpenWeatherMap).

6.2. Setting Up the HTML Structure

index.html:

html

```
<!DOCTYPE html>
<html lang="en">
<head>
  <meta charset="UTF-8">
  <title>Real-Time Weather App</title>
  <link rel="stylesheet" href="styles.css">
</head>
<body>
  <section class="weather-app">
```

```
<h1>Weather Dashboard</h1>
<div class="search-bar">
  <input type="text" id="cityInput"
placeholder="Enter city">
  <button id="searchBtn">Get Weather</button>
</div>


<div class="weather-info" id="weatherInfo">
  <!-- Weather details will appear here -->
  <p class="message">Search for a city to see
the weather.</p>
</div>
</section>


<script src="app.js"></script>
</body>
</html>
```

- The user types a **city** in the <input>.

- Clicks **"Get Weather"** or presses Enter.

- The **weather-info** section updates with temperature, icon, and conditions.

6.3. Styling the Weather Dashboard

styles.css (a simple example):

```css
css


body {
  margin: 0;
  font-family: Arial, sans-serif;
  background: #f2f2f2;
}


.weather-app {
  max-width: 500px;
  margin: 50px auto;
  text-align: center;
  background: #fff;
  padding: 20px;
  border-radius: 8px;
}


.search-bar {
  display: flex;
  justify-content: center;
  margin-bottom: 20px;
}


#cityInput {
  width: 60%;
  padding: 10px;
```

```css
  border: 1px solid #ccc;
  border-radius: 4px 0 0 4px;
}


#searchBtn {
  padding: 10px 20px;
  border: none;
  background: #007BFF;
  color: #fff;
  border-radius: 0 4px 4px 0;
  cursor: pointer;
}


#searchBtn:hover {
  background: #0056b3;
}


.weather-info {
  margin-top: 20px;
}

.message {
  color: #666;
}
```

We've created a centered card-like container. The search bar has an input and a button side by side.

6.4. Integrating the Fetch API for Weather Data

app.js:

```javascript

document.addEventListener("DOMContentLoaded", ()
=> {
  const cityInput =
document.getElementById("cityInput");
  const searchBtn =
document.getElementById("searchBtn");
  const weatherInfo =
document.getElementById("weatherInfo");

  // Replace with your actual OpenWeatherMap API
key
  const API_KEY = "YOUR_OPENWEATHERMAP_API_KEY";

  searchBtn.addEventListener("click", () => {
    const city = cityInput.value.trim();
    if (city) {
      getWeather(city);
    } else {
      displayMessage("Please enter a city name.");
    }
  });
```

```javascript
// Press Enter to search
cityInput.addEventListener("keypress", (e) => {
  if (e.key === "Enter") {
    const city = cityInput.value.trim();
    if (city) {
      getWeather(city);
    } else {
      displayMessage("Please enter a city
name.");
    }
  }
});


function getWeather(city) {
  const url =
`https://api.openweathermap.org/data/2.5/weather?q
=${city}&units=metric&appid=${API_KEY}`;

  fetch(url)
    .then(response => {
      if (!response.ok) {
        throw new Error(`Error:
${response.status} ${response.statusText}`);
      }
      return response.json();
```

```
    })
    .then(data => {
      // Extract relevant info
      const { main, name, weather } = data;
      const temperature = main.temp;
      const condition = weather[0].description;
      const iconId = weather[0].icon; // e.g.,
"04n"


      updateWeatherUI(name, temperature,
condition, iconId);
    })
    .catch(err => {
      displayMessage(`Failed to fetch weather
data. ${err.message}`);
    });
  }


  function updateWeatherUI(cityName, temp,
condition, iconId) {
    const iconUrl =
`https://openweathermap.org/img/wn/${iconId}@2x.pn
g`;


    weatherInfo.innerHTML = `
    <h2>${cityName}</h2>
```

```
    <img src="${iconUrl}" alt="Weather icon">
    <p>${temp}°C - ${condition}</p>
  `;

}


function displayMessage(msg) {
  weatherInfo.innerHTML = `<p
class="message">${msg}</p>`;
  }
});
```

Explanation:

- We add event listeners to both the **Search** button and the **Enter** key on the input, calling getWeather(city).

- In getWeather, we construct the API URL with **metric** units (Celsius) and the appid for authentication.

- We call fetch(url). If the response is not OK (e.g., city not found), we throw an error. Otherwise, we parse it as JSON.

- In updateWeatherUI, we dynamically inject the city name, temperature, and an icon representing the conditions.

- If something fails (invalid city, no network, etc.), catch displays a message instead of crashing.

6.5. Updating the UI Dynamically

Because we're not reloading the page, the user can try multiple cities, each time seeing immediate results. This is the essence of AJAX: partial updates without full page reload.

6.6. Adding Error Handling and Edge Cases

1. **Empty city**: We call displayMessage("Please enter a city name.").

2. **Unknown city**: The server might return a 404 or 400, prompting an error message.

3. **Network offline**: The .catch block handles it, informing the user.

4. **Rate Limits**: If the user tries too many requests in a short time, the API might reject requests. We can respond accordingly.

6.7. Potential Enhancements

- **Geolocation**: Detect user location automatically.

- **Autocomplete**: Suggest city names as the user types.

- **7-Day Forecast**: Another endpoint from the API could show extended forecasts.

- **Local Storage**: Remember the last searched city.

7. AJAX Patterns and Best Practices

7.1. Optimizing Network Requests

- **Batch Requests:** Instead of sending one request per keypress in live search, wait until the user stops typing.

- **Caching:** If your data is static or rarely changes, store it locally so repeated visits don't re-fetch the same info.

- **Pagination:** For large datasets, fetch only what's needed, then fetch more as the user scrolls.

7.2. Caching Strategies and Local Storage

For instance, if your app fetches the same config data multiple times, store the results in a variable or **localStorage**. Next time, load from there instead of hitting the API again. This approach can drastically speed up your app and reduce server load.

7.3. Avoiding Callback Hell with Promises/Async-Await

Nested callbacks can become unreadable quickly. With the **Fetch API**, you can chain .then() calls. Alternatively, use the more synchronous-looking **async/await**:

```javascript
async function fetchData(url) {
  try {
    const response = await fetch(url);
    if (!response.ok) {
      throw new Error(`HTTP error! status:
${response.status}`);
    }
    const data = await response.json();
    console.log(data);
  } catch (error) {
    console.error("Fetch error:", error);
  }
}
```

This approach simplifies complex logic flows, especially if you have multiple sequential requests.

7.4. Handling Rate Limits and API Quotas

Public APIs often impose **rate limits**—the maximum number of requests per second/day. Handle them by:

- **Backing Off**: If you receive HTTP 429 (Too Many Requests), wait a short time before retrying.

- **Minimal Requests**: Combine multiple data needs into a single request if possible.

- **Clever Caching**: Don't re-request data that's unlikely to have changed.

---

8. Security Considerations and Cross-Domain Requests

8.1. The Same-Origin Policy and CORS

By default, browsers enforce the **Same-Origin Policy**, restricting scripts from making requests to a different domain. **CORS** (Cross-Origin Resource Sharing) is a mechanism that allows servers to explicitly permit cross-domain requests via special headers like:

arduino

Access-Control-Allow-Origin: https://yourdomain.com

If the server doesn't set these headers, your client-side fetch to that domain might fail due to browser security rules.

8.2. Dealing with Preflight Requests

Certain requests (like PUT, DELETE, or custom headers) trigger a **preflight** OPTIONS request to confirm the server's CORS policy. Understand that some calls may do a preflight before the actual request.

8.3. CSRF and XSS Concerns in Asynchronous Calls

Asynchronous calls are susceptible to the same vulnerabilities as synchronous requests:

- **CSRF (Cross-Site Request Forgery)**: Attackers can trick a logged-in user's browser into performing actions on another site. Solutions include **CSRF tokens** or checking custom headers.

- **XSS (Cross-Site Scripting)**: If you inject untrusted data (like user-generated content) into the page, it could contain malicious scripts. Always sanitize or encode data before insertion.

9. Debugging and Testing Asynchronous Code

9.1. Browser DevTools for Network Analysis

Most browsers provide a **Network** tab where you can see each request, its URL, status code, timing, and response. This is invaluable for diagnosing slow calls, verifying request/response headers, or checking that your data structure is as expected.

9.2. Console Logs, Breakpoints, and the Performance Tab

Strategic console.log() statements help you see the flow of data. Alternatively, set breakpoints in your code to pause execution and inspect variables in real time. The **Performance** tab can show how your asynchronous calls affect rendering and CPU usage.

9.3. Mocking APIs in Automated Tests

For robust testing, you might not want to depend on a live API. Tools like **Jest**, **Mocha**, or **Cypress** allow you to **mock fetch** calls. This way, you can test your logic (parsing, UI updates, error handling) without requiring an external network.

10. Advanced Topics

10.1. Streaming Responses and the ReadableStream Interface

The **Fetch** API supports streaming responses, letting you process data chunks as they arrive rather than waiting for the entire response. This is beneficial for large files or real-time feeds (though for truly real-time, you might consider WebSockets).

10.2. AbortController for Canceling Fetch Requests

Sometimes you need to cancel a request—e.g., the user navigates away or changes their input before the response arrives. The **AbortController** allows you to do:

javascript

```javascript
const controller = new AbortController();
fetch(url, { signal: controller.signal });
controller.abort(); // Cancels the fetch
```

10.3. WebSockets and Real-Time Communication

While AJAX/Fetch provide request-response flows, **WebSockets** enable persistent connections for real-time data pushes from server to client. This is ideal for chat apps, multiplayer games, or real-time dashboards. However, the fundamental principles of asynchronous handling remain similar.

10.4. GraphQL and Other Modern Alternatives

Instead of REST or REST-like APIs, many modern apps use **GraphQL**. This can reduce multiple round trips by letting clients request exactly the data shape they need. Nonetheless, the actual fetching mechanism still typically relies on the same asynchronous approaches—using fetch, or specialized GraphQL clients that wrap fetch under the hood.

---

11. Conclusion

AJAX revolutionized the web by **decoupling** data fetches from page loads, laying the groundwork for the interactive, fluid experiences we take for granted today. With the shift from XMLHttpRequest to the **Fetch API**, developers now enjoy a more elegant, promise-based interface to retrieve JSON, submit forms, and handle errors seamlessly. This approach turns the web from a collection of static pages into dynamic, app-like environments that respond instantly to user input.

Key Takeaways

1. **Asynchronous Mindset**: Embrace the fact that calls happen in the background. Write code that updates only when the data is ready, preventing blocking on the main thread.

2. **Fetch API**: Offers a modern syntax, promise-based error handling, and straightforward JSON parsing.

3. **Error Handling**: Always consider non-OK status codes and network failures.

4. **Real-World Integration**: Our weather app exemplifies how easy it is to query external APIs, parse data, and update the UI dynamically.

5. **Security and CORS**: Understand the browser's same-origin policy, use server-side headers for cross-origin requests, and remain vigilant about CSRF/XSS.

6. **Performance and Testing**: Use DevTools to measure performance, mock APIs in tests, and cache responses to reduce load times.

By mastering these techniques, you can build richer, more engaging websites that load new data on demand instead of forcing full-page refreshes. Whether you're implementing live feeds, auto-updating dashboards, interactive forms, or full-scale single-page applications, **AJAX** and **Fetch** remain at the heart of the modern web, giving developers the power to create experiences that delight users, day in and day out.

Chapter 11: Introduction to Front-End Frameworks: React and Vue

---

1. The Evolution of Front-End Development

The days of static HTML files and simple JavaScript snippets are long behind us. In the modern web landscape, user interfaces must be **fast, responsive**, and **highly dynamic**, often interfacing with real-time data streams and advanced APIs. As user expectations soared for rich experiences akin to native apps, front-end developers found themselves juggling complex state management, frequent UI updates, and code that grew unwieldy with scale.

It was from these challenges that **front-end frameworks** such as **React** and **Vue** emerged. These libraries and frameworks introduced strategies for:

- **Encapsulating UI logic** into distinct components.

- **Maintaining predictable state management** within and across components.

- **Making incremental updates** to the user interface without reloading entire pages.

React and Vue in particular have garnered massive developer communities. Both adopt a **component-centric** philosophy, meaning your UI is divided into self-contained building blocks, each handling its own data and rendering logic. These building blocks can be composed into complex interfaces, effectively managing the increasing demands of modern web applications.

In this chapter, we'll explore **why** front-end frameworks have become so prevalent, examine the **core features** of both React and Vue, and walk through building a **simple interactive application in React**. By the end, you'll have a clearer grasp of how these frameworks streamline development, what sets them apart, and how they can serve as a foundation for your next project.

---

2. Why Use Front-End Frameworks?

2.1. The Complexities of Modern Web Apps

In earlier eras, a typical site displayed static pages sprinkled with a bit of JavaScript or jQuery for basic interactivity. Now, consider how many sites:

1. **Render dynamic data in real time** (e.g., dashboards, live feeds).

2. **Handle user interactions** across multiple features (like e-commerce checkouts, in-app notifications, or chat interfaces).

3. **Maintain state** seamlessly when users navigate from one view to another, or when they revisit a page.

4. **Support offline and partial offline modes** with caching and service workers.

Managing these tasks with vanilla JavaScript alone is possible but becomes extremely cumbersome. Each new feature can significantly complicate the codebase. This leads to fragile code, difficult debugging, and a high barrier for new developers joining the project.

2.2. Simplifying State Management and UI Updates

Front-end frameworks like React and Vue provide a structured approach to data flow and UI reactivity:

- **Declarative Rendering:** Instead of manually manipulating the DOM, you declare **how** the UI should look based on data. When the data changes, the framework updates the DOM automatically in an efficient manner.

- **One-Way or Two-Way Data Binding:** React typically uses **one-way** data flow, which can prevent confusion about where changes originate. Vue supports **two-way** binding out of the box (though it also encourages one-way flows for clarity). Both approaches reduce the overhead of manually synchronizing data changes in multiple places.

- **Predictable State Management**: Through recommended patterns (like Redux in React or Vuex in Vue), you can store application data in centralized objects, ensuring that each UI component reflects only the slice of the state relevant to it.

2.3. Benefits of React, Vue, and Other Frameworks

- **Reusability**: Components are modular and self-contained, so you can quickly assemble multiple pages or sections from the same building blocks.

- **Performance**: Both React and Vue use **virtual DOM** rendering, applying minimal changes to the real DOM as data updates, greatly improving speed over naive solutions.

- **Ecosystem and Community**: Each framework has a robust collection of libraries, tools, and best practices. Whether you're building forms, charts, or routes, you'll find well-tested solutions.

- **Developer Experience**: Tools like create-react-app, Vue CLI, Hot Module Reloading, DevTools integration, and typed support with TypeScript make it far simpler to build, test, and debug applications.

---

3. React Basics

3.1. The Philosophy Behind React

React was developed by Facebook (now Meta) around 2013. Its core philosophy is **"learn once, write anywhere."** React focuses on **building user interfaces**—it's not a complete solution for routing, form handling, or state management. Instead, it's a **library** (often mislabeled as a "framework") that pairs well with other libraries to form a comprehensive stack.

React introduced the **virtual DOM** concept to mainstream front-end development. When data changes, React compares the new UI description with the old one, figuring out the minimum set of DOM operations to apply. This approach significantly improves performance compared to naive DOM manipulations.

3.2. Components: The Building Blocks of a React App

In React, everything is a **component**. A component can be a **function** or **class** that returns a snippet of **JSX** (JavaScript XML). For example:

```jsx

function Greeting(props) {
  return <h1>Hello, {props.name}!</h1>;
}
```

Each component:

1. **Takes in data** (props) as an input.

2. **Outputs a rendered UI** (JSX).

3. May or may not manage its own internal **state**.

Components can be nested within each other, forming a tree-like structure. This fosters reusability: once you define a **Button** component, you can use <Button /> in many places, passing in different props.

3.3. Props: Passing Data Between Components

Props (short for properties) are how React components receive input from a parent:

jsx

```jsx
function App() {
  return (
    <div>
      <Greeting name="Alice" />
      <Greeting name="Bob" />
    </div>
  );
}
```

Here, <Greeting name="Alice" /> passes a prop called name with the value "Alice" to the Greeting component. Inside Greeting, we can access it via props.name. Props in React are **read-only**—a component should never directly modify its props. This immutability helps maintain predictable data flows.

3.4. State: Managing Dynamic Data

While props come from parents, **state** is managed **within** a component itself. A component's state can change over time, usually in response to user interactions or network responses. With React Hooks, we use:

jsx

```jsx
import { useState } from "react";

function Counter() {
  const [count, setCount] = useState(0);

  return (
    <div>
      <p>You clicked {count} times</p>
      <button onClick={() => setCount(count + 1)}>
        Increment
      </button>
    </div>
  );
}
```

- useState(0) creates a state variable count and a function setCount.

- Clicking the button calls setCount(count + 1), which re-renders the component with the updated value.

Stateful components let you build interactive UIs. The data flow remains mostly unidirectional: changes happen in a child or parent, and that triggers a re-render, updating the UI accordingly.

3.5. Lifecycle Methods and Hooks (Brief Overview)

Before React Hooks, class components used **lifecycle methods** like componentDidMount, componentDidUpdate, and componentWillUnmount. Modern React encourages **functional components with Hooks** instead, such as:

- **useEffect:** Replaces lifecycle methods for side effects, like fetching data or subscribing to events.

- **useContext:** Access global data without passing props manually down multiple levels.

- **useReducer:** Manage more complex state transitions in a functional manner, reminiscent of Redux.

Though these concepts go beyond the basics, they highlight how React addresses real-world needs like asynchronous data fetching, resource cleanup, and state management in a manner that's maintainable and consistent.

4. Vue.js Basics

4.1. The Progressive Framework

Vue.js was created by Evan You, who had worked on AngularJS at Google. Vue's tagline is **"The Progressive Framework,"** meaning you can adopt it incrementally. It's not an all-or-nothing approach: you can drop a <script> tag into an existing page to handle small interactivity, or you can build an entire single-page application (SPA) with advanced tooling.

Vue aims to combine the best features of Angular (like declarative templates and easy reactivity) with the performance and flexibility of React's Virtual DOM. The result is a **lightweight** and **approachable** framework that new developers often find quick to learn.

4.2. Template Syntax and Directives

A hallmark of Vue is its **HTML-based template syntax.** Consider a simple component:

```html
<template>
  <div>
    <p>Hello, {{ name }}!</p>
```

```
    <button @click="changeName">Change
Name</button>
  </div>
</template>

<script>
export default {
  data() {
    return {
      name: "Alice"
    }
  },
  methods: {
    changeName() {
      this.name = "Bob"
    }
  }
}
</script>
```

- The <template> block is written similarly to regular HTML, but with **Vue directives** (like v-if, v-for, or @click).

- **Interpolations** ({{ name }}) insert dynamic values into the template.

- The <script> block defines the component's logic: data and methods.

- **data()** returns an object with local reactive properties. In the example, name is initially "Alice". Changing this.name to "Bob" automatically re-renders the template.

4.3. Reactive Data and Computed Properties

Vue automatically tracks changes to data within a component, updating the DOM as needed. This is known as Vue's **reactive system**. Additionally, Vue supports **computed properties**, which are cached until their dependencies change:

html

```html
<template>
  <div>
    <p>Full Name: {{ fullName }}</p>
  </div>
</template>

<script>
export default {
  data() {
    return {
      firstName: "Alice",
```

```
    lastName: "Johnson"
  }
},
computed: {
  fullName() {
    return this.firstName + " " + this.lastName
  }
}
}
</script>
```

fullName will only re-calculate if firstName or lastName changes, avoiding unnecessary re-render overhead.

4.4. Components in Vue

Like React, Vue encourages you to break your app into smaller pieces:

html

```html
<!-- Parent component -->
<template>
  <div>
    <child-component :user="loggedInUser" />
  </div>
</template>
```

```
<script>
import ChildComponent from "./ChildComponent.vue";

export default {
  components: { ChildComponent },
  data() {
    return { loggedInUser: { name: "Alice" } }
  }
}
</script>
```

In the child:

html

```
<template>
  <div>
    <p>Hello, {{ user.name }}!</p>
  </div>
</template>

<script>
export default {
  props: ["user"]
}
</script>
```

The parent passes the loggedInUser object down as a prop called user. Vue handles reactivity and keeps everything in sync.

4.5. Vue's Approach to State Management

For larger apps, Vue has an official state management library called **Vuex**. The concept is akin to Redux in React, storing a single source of truth for app-wide data. Components commit mutations to the store, which triggers an update for any subscribed components. This ensures consistent and debuggable data flows as your project scales.

---

5. Comparing React and Vue

5.1. Similarities: Virtual DOM, Reusability, and More

- **Virtual DOM**: Both React and Vue maintain a virtual DOM, updating only what's necessary in the real DOM.

- **Component Architecture**: UIs are divided into smaller, reusable components with props for data input.

- **Unidirectional Data Flow** (by default): Encourages clarity in how changes propagate.

- **Ecosystem**: Each has a robust ecosystem of libraries, devtools, and community resources.

5.2. Differences in Syntax and Philosophy

- **Template vs. JSX**: Vue uses an **HTML-based template** syntax by default, with directives for loops, conditionals, and event listeners. React uses **JSX**, mixing JavaScript logic directly into markup.

- **Two-Way Binding**: Vue makes two-way binding (v-model) straightforward, especially for forms. React tends to rely on unidirectional data flow, though you can emulate two-way patterns.

- **Complexity**: React is minimal at the core but often requires multiple libraries for routing, state management, etc. Vue provides a more integrated approach, including official solutions for routing (Vue Router) and state management (Vuex).

5.3. Ecosystem and Community Support

- **React**: Extremely popular in enterprise settings. A vast ecosystem, including libraries like React Router, Redux, and Material UI.

- **Vue**: Rapidly growing community, widespread adoption in Asia, and known for approachability. Offers official solutions like Vue Router, Vuex, and a CLI that streamlines scaffolding.

Ultimately, both frameworks can handle complex applications at scale. Choosing one often comes down to team preference, existing codebase needs, or project timelines.

---

6. Real-World Example: Building a Simple Interactive Application using React

6.1. Project Overview and Goals

Let's build a basic **"To-Do"** style application where users can:

1. **Add** new tasks.

2. **Mark tasks** as completed or not completed.

3. **Filter** tasks (e.g., show all, show only active tasks, show only completed tasks).

We'll keep the UI minimal but highlight React's core patterns:

props, state, events, and **conditional rendering**.

6.2. Setting Up the Environment (Node, Create React App)

Assuming you have **Node.js** installed:

1. **Install create-react-app:**

bash

```
npx create-react-app todo-app
```

2. **Navigate** to the new folder:

bash

```bash
cd todo-app
```

3. **Start** the development server:

```bash
bash
```

```bash
npm start
```

This scaffolds a React app with default files. The dev server runs at http://localhost:3000, reloading automatically as you edit code.

6.3. Structuring Your React Project

Inside src/, you'll see:

- **App.js**: The root App component.

- **index.js**: Entry point that renders <App /> to the DOM.

We'll create:

- **components/TaskList.js**: Displays a list of tasks.

- **components/TaskItem.js**: Represents a single task.

- Possibly a **components/FilterButtons.js** for toggling the filter state.

6.4. Creating and Styling the Main Components

App.js (initial version):

```jsx
jsx
```

```
import React, { useState } from "react";
import TaskList from "./components/TaskList";
import "./App.css";

function App() {
  const [tasks, setTasks] = useState([
    { id: 1, text: "Learn React", completed: false
},
    { id: 2, text: "Build a To-Do App", completed:
false },
    { id: 3, text: "Celebrate!", completed: false
}
  ]);

  return (
    <div className="app-container">
      <h1>React To-Do</h1>
      <TaskList tasks={tasks} setTasks={setTasks}
/>
    </div>
  );
}

export default App;
```

- We manage tasks as state in the **parent** (App).

- Pass tasks and setTasks down to <TaskList />.

TaskList.js:

jsx

```jsx
import React from "react";
import TaskItem from "./TaskItem";

export default function TaskList({ tasks, setTasks
}) {
  return (
    <div>
      {tasks.map(task => (
        <TaskItem
          key={task.id}
          task={task}
          setTasks={setTasks}
        />
      ))}
    </div>
  );
}
```

TaskItem.js:

jsx

```
import React from "react";

export default function TaskItem({ task, setTasks
}) {
  const handleToggle = () => {
    // update the completed state for this task
    setTasks(prevTasks =>
      prevTasks.map(t =>
        t.id === task.id ? { ...t, completed:
!t.completed } : t
      )
    );
  };


  return (
    <div style={{ marginBottom: "8px" }}>
      <input
        type="checkbox"
        checked={task.completed}
        onChange={handleToggle}
      />
      <span style={{
        textDecoration: task.completed ? "line-
through" : "none",
        marginLeft: "8px"
      }}>
```

```
      {task.text}
    </span>
  </div>
);
}
```

When the user checks or unchecks the box, handleToggle updates the relevant task in the parent's state, toggling completed.

Styling in App.css might be minimal:

css

```css
.app-container {
  max-width: 400px;
  margin: 0 auto;
  padding: 20px;
  font-family: Arial, sans-serif;
}


h1 {
  text-align: center;
}
```

6.5. Managing State and Props in Practice

Notice the **unidirectional data flow**:

1. App holds the array of tasks in state.

2. It passes tasks and setTasks to TaskList.

3. TaskList loops over tasks, rendering TaskItem.

4. TaskItem modifies a specific task by calling setTasks.

React re-renders as soon as the state changes, so the UI always displays up-to-date task data.

6.6. Adding Interactivity (Event Handling and Hooks)

Let's implement the ability to **add a new task** in App.js:

jsx

```
function App() {
  const [tasks, setTasks] = useState([...]);
  const [newTaskText, setNewTaskText] =
useState("");

  const addTask = e => {
    e.preventDefault();
    if (!newTaskText.trim()) return;
    const newTask = {
      id: Date.now(),
      text: newTaskText,
      completed: false
```

```
    };
    setTasks(prev => [...prev, newTask]);
    setNewTaskText("");
  };

  return (
    <div className="app-container">
      <h1>React To-Do</h1>
      <form onSubmit={addTask}>
        <input
          type="text"
          value={newTaskText}
          onChange={e =>
setNewTaskText(e.target.value)}
          placeholder="What needs to be done?"
        />
        <button type="submit">Add</button>
      </form>
      <TaskList tasks={tasks} setTasks={setTasks}
/>
    </div>
  );
}
```

- newTaskText stores the text for the new task.

- Submitting the form triggers addTask, which creates a new object and appends it to tasks.

- Date.now() is a quick way to generate a unique ID, though real apps might use UUID or server-generated IDs.

6.7. Testing, Debugging, and Deployment

1. **Testing**: React tests often use Jest and React Testing Library. You could test if your App renders tasks, if TaskItem toggles the checkbox, etc.

2. **Debugging**: The React DevTools browser extension helps inspect component hierarchies, props, and state.

3. **Deployment**: A production build with npm run build creates optimized static files in build/. You can deploy them to services like Netlify, Vercel, or your own server.

---

7. Transitioning from React to Vue (and Vice Versa)

7.1. Adapting Mental Models

- In **React**, you think in terms of **JSX** and functional or class components. Data flow is mostly **one-way**.

- In **Vue**, you deal with **templates** and "options objects" that define data, computed properties, watchers, etc.

Moving from one to the other requires adjusting how you handle templates, event binding, and state management patterns. However, the concept of "split the UI into small, reusable components" remains consistent.

7.2. Rewriting Components and Data Flows

If you have a React codebase and want to try Vue, or vice versa, you'll likely rewrite the components in the other framework's syntax. The underlying logic (like how you structure data or handle events) can remain, but the way you declare them changes. It's also possible to progressively integrate Vue into an existing React app or vice versa, but that's more specialized and typically not recommended unless you have a strong reason.

7.3. Tips for Multilingual Codebases

- **Maintain separate modules** or files for each framework's components.

- **Refactor shared logic** into pure JavaScript utility libraries that can be used by both frameworks.

- **Gradual migration**: If you have a large codebase in React, you might rewrite specific pieces in Vue. Keep them separate to avoid confusion.

---

8. Performance Considerations

8.1. Optimizing React with Memo, PureComponent, and Code Splitting

- **React.memo**: Wrap functional components to skip re-renders if props haven't changed.

- **PureComponent**: For class components, automatically does a shallow comparison of props and state to decide if a re-render is needed.

- **Code Splitting**: Tools like React.lazy and Suspense load parts of your app only when needed, improving initial load times.

8.2. Vue's Reactivity System and Lazy Loading

Vue's reactivity is built around watchers and proxies. For performance-critical apps:

- **v-once** or **v-memo** can ensure certain parts of the template never re-render after initial render.

- **Dynamic imports** can break the app into smaller chunks, loaded only when the user navigates to a particular route or triggers a certain feature.

8.3. Avoiding Unnecessary Renders

Both frameworks strive to minimize direct DOM manipulations. However, you can still degrade performance if you do large calculations within each render cycle or cause large subtrees to update too often. Keep an eye on what changes trigger re-renders, and isolate or memoize expensive computations.

---

9. Best Practices and Future Trends

9.1. Maintainable Code Architecture

- **Use file/folder structures** that group related components and styles, e.g., components/, pages/, store/.

- **Name components** and their files consistently (e.g., PascalCase or kebab-case).

- **Document** your props, states, and data flows. Tools like **Storybook** can help visualize and test components in isolation.

9.2. TypeScript Integration

Both React and Vue support **TypeScript**, which helps catch errors early and provide better tooling for large-scale projects. For React, you might create .tsx files with typed props; for Vue, you can combine single-file components with TypeScript.

9.3. The Rise of Server Components and SSR

- **Server-Side Rendering (SSR)**: Tools like **Next.js** (React) or **Nuxt.js** (Vue) pre-render pages on the server for better SEO and faster initial load.

- **Server Components**: An experimental React feature that allows certain components to render on the server side, reducing the client's JavaScript bundle.

9.4. Evolving Framework Ecosystems (Next.js, Nuxt.js, etc.)

- **Next.js**: A popular React framework providing built-in SSR, file-based routing, and incremental static regeneration.

- **Nuxt.js**: Vue's counterpart for SSR and static site generation, boasting easy configuration and performance boosts.

As these frameworks mature, you'll see more synergy between server and client code, likely leading to a future where large, complex apps can be optimized out-of-the-box for performance, SEO, and developer productivity.

---

10. Conclusion

Front-end frameworks like **React** and **Vue** have transformed the way we build dynamic web applications, providing:

- **Scalable architectures** for complex UIs.

- **Efficient re-rendering** via virtual DOMs.

- **Declarative data binding** to minimize manual DOM manipulation.

We explored the **core principles**—components, props, state, reactivity—through the lens of both frameworks and showcased a **real-world React example** of a to-do application. Though their syntax and philosophies differ in some places, both React and Vue champion the idea of **breaking down the UI into modular, reusable elements**, simplifying the complexity of modern web development.

Key Takeaways:

1. **Frameworks Address Complexity**: They solve state synchronization challenges, promote best practices, and streamline rendering performance.

2. **React**: Emphasizes a minimal, component-based approach with JSX. Great for large-scale apps that need ultimate flexibility, especially with a massive ecosystem.

3. **Vue**: Balances approachability with depth. Its template syntax is intuitive, making it easy for teams from different backgrounds to adopt.

4. **Community and Ecosystem**: Whether you choose React or Vue, you'll find robust documentation, libraries, devtools, and a large community.

5. **Future Trends**: SSR, server components, TypeScript, and performance optimizations will shape how we build the front-end in the coming years.

Ultimately, whether you opt for React or Vue often depends on your team's preferences, project requirements, or existing codebases. Each library can handle everything from small interactive widgets to massive single-page applications. By understanding their fundamentals and applying best practices, you'll be well-prepared to deliver fast, maintainable, and user-friendly web interfaces that stand the test of time.

Chapter 12: Building and Integrating Python APIs with Flask

---

1. Introduction

Modern web applications demand seamless communication between client-side interfaces and back-end logic. Whether you're building a single-page application (SPA), a mobile app, or a data-driven service, you'll likely need an **application programming interface (API)** to interact with your server-side code. On the Python side, **Flask** has become one of the most popular microframeworks for quickly spinning up robust and maintainable APIs.

In this chapter, we'll walk through everything you need to know to **build and integrate a Python-based API** using Flask. We'll start by understanding what an API is in today's tech landscape, then delve into how Flask simplifies the process of creating and managing RESTful endpoints. You'll learn best practices for organizing your Flask project, returning JSON responses, handling errors, and exposing data to the front-end. Finally, we'll walk through a **real-world example**: a user-management API that our JavaScript front-end will consume to display and update user data dynamically in the browser.

By the end of this chapter, you'll be equipped to **design, implement, and deploy** a Flask-based API that can be accessed by virtually any client—whether it's a React web interface, a Vue single-page app, or even a mobile application. Let's dive in.

---

2. What Is an API?

2.1. The Role of APIs in Modern Applications

An **API** is a contract or interface that defines how different pieces of software communicate with each other. Instead of merging codebases or requiring the front-end to know the details of how the back-end logic works, the API provides a **clean, standardized layer** for requests and responses.

Consider a mobile app that needs to fetch user profiles, upload pictures, or retrieve analytics data. Rather than embedding all the logic in the client, that app can make **HTTP requests** to a server endpoint that is documented via an API. The server processes those requests, interacts with databases or other services as needed, and returns relevant data in a consistent format—often **JSON**.

2.2. Common API Architectures and Protocols

While older protocols like XML-RPC or SOAP still exist, the majority of web APIs today follow **RESTful** (Representational State Transfer) principles. Common characteristics of RESTful APIs include:

1. **Resource-Based URLs**: E.g., /users/123 to reference a specific user.

2. **HTTP Methods**: GET, POST, PUT, PATCH, DELETE, etc. each serve a semantic purpose.

3. **Stateless Interactions**: Each request contains all the data the server needs, independent of prior requests.

4. **JSON** as a primary data format (though not strictly required).

Beyond REST, you might also encounter **GraphQL**, which allows clients to define precisely the data shape they want, or real-time systems like **WebSockets**. For most typical back-end services, a RESTful JSON-based approach remains the simplest and most widely adopted.

2.3. RESTful Principles vs. Other API Paradigms

- **REST**: Encourages resources, consistent methods, and statelessness.

- **GraphQL**: A query language for APIs, flexible but more complex to implement.

- **gRPC**: Uses protocol buffers for fast, compact data transport, often favored for internal microservices or high-performance scenarios.

Our focus here is on a **REST-like approach** using Flask's routing and JSON responses. This approach is widely compatible with any front-end: from vanilla JavaScript or React to mobile platforms like iOS or Android.

---

3. Flask API Basics

3.1. What Is Flask, and Why Use It for APIs?

Flask is a **Python microframework** that excels in simplicity and flexibility:

1. **Minimal Boilerplate**: You can start a basic Flask app with just a few lines of code.

2. **Extensible**: You can add only the libraries you need—like SQLAlchemy for databases or Marshmallow for data serialization—rather than dealing with a monolithic framework.

3. **Large Ecosystem**: Flask has a huge community, many extensions, and thorough documentation.

4. **Lightweight**: Perfect for microservices or small to medium APIs, yet it scales well with the right architecture.

3.2. Setting Up Your Flask Environment

To get started:

1. **Install Python 3.7+** (preferably from python.org or your system's package manager).

2. Create a **virtual environment** (recommended) to isolate your dependencies:

bash

```
python -m venv venv
source venv/bin/activate  # Mac/Linux
# or venv\Scripts\activate on Windows
```

3. **Install Flask**:

bash

```
pip install Flask
```

4. **Verify** your installation by opening a Python shell:

```
python
```

```
import flask
print(flask.__version__)
```

3.3. Creating Your First Flask Endpoint

Let's create a minimal app.py:

```python

from flask import Flask

app = Flask(__name__)

@app.route('/')
def hello_world():
    return 'Hello, Flask!'

if __name__ == '__main__':
    app.run(debug=True)
```

- We import Flask and instantiate the app with Flask(__name__).

- The @app.route('/') decorator maps the root URL / to the function hello_world.

- app.run(debug=True) starts the development server in debug mode, so it automatically reloads on code changes.

Visit http://127.0.0.1:5000/ in your browser, and you'll see **Hello, Flask!**.

3.4. Handling Routes, Methods, and Status Codes

APIs typically accept various **HTTP methods**:

- **GET**: Retrieve data (read-only).

- **POST**: Create new data.

- **PUT/PATCH**: Update existing data.

- **DELETE**: Remove data.

In Flask:

python

```
@app.route('/api/users', methods=['GET'])
def list_users():
    return {'users': [...]}, 200
```

1. methods=['GET'] ensures this endpoint only responds to GET requests.

2. You can return a tuple (data, status_code). Flask automatically tries to convert data to an HTTP response.

3.5. JSON Serialization and the Flask jsonify Utility

While returning a Python dictionary automatically turns it into JSON, many developers prefer **jsonify** for consistency:

python

```python
from flask import jsonify


@app.route('/api/users/<int:user_id>',
methods=['GET'])
def get_user(user_id):
    user = find_user_in_database(user_id)
    if not user:
        return jsonify({'error': 'User not
found'}), 404

    return jsonify({'id': user.id, 'name':
user.name, 'email': user.email}), 200
```

jsonify ensures the response has the correct MIME type (application/json) and handles some edge cases. You could also manually return json.dumps(...), but jsonify is the canonical Flask approach.

4. Designing a Well-Structured Python API

4.1. Folder Structures and Blueprints

As your API grows, a single app.py can become messy. Flask **blueprints** let you split functionalities into modules:

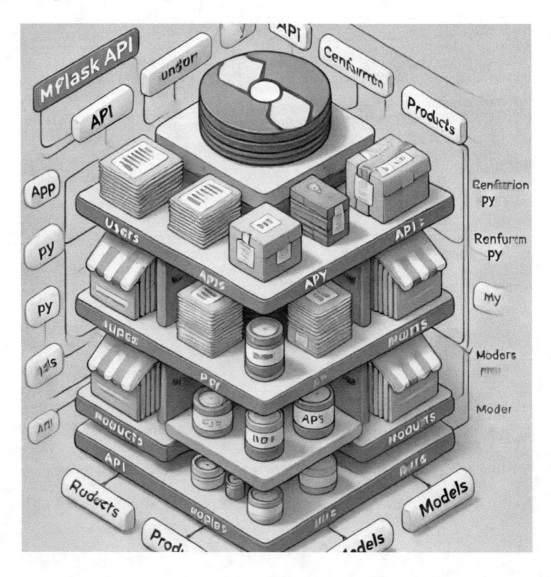

- Each Python file inside api/ might define routes relevant to that domain (e.g., user management).

- Blueprints can be registered in app.py:

```python

from api.users import users_bp
...
app.register_blueprint(users_bp,
url_prefix='/api')
```

4.2. Configuration Management and Environment Variables

Use a config.py or environment variables to store secrets like database credentials, API keys, or debug flags. For instance:

```python

import os

class Config:
    DEBUG = os.getenv('FLASK_DEBUG', False)
    SECRET_KEY = os.getenv('SECRET_KEY',
'change_this')

class DevelopmentConfig(Config):
```

```
    DEBUG = True


class ProductionConfig(Config):
    DEBUG = False
```

In app.py:

python

```
app.config.from_object('config.DevelopmentConfig')
```

Later, switching to production is as simple as referencing ProductionConfig or adjusting environment variables.

4.3. Database Connections and ORM Options

For data persistence, you might use:

- **SQLite**: Perfect for small projects or quick prototypes.

- **PostgreSQL** or **MySQL**: Common for production environments.

- **SQLAlchemy**: A powerful ORM that integrates well with Flask.

- **NoSQL** solutions like MongoDB (via PyMongo) if your data model is highly flexible.

4.4. Error Handling and Custom Responses

Create custom error handlers:

```python
@app.errorhandler(404)
def not_found(e):
    return jsonify({'error': 'Not Found'}), 404


@app.errorhandler(500)
def server_error(e):
    return jsonify({'error': 'Internal Server
Error'}), 500
```

This ensures consistent JSON responses for unexpected scenarios. You can also define custom exceptions if you want more granular error reporting.

4.5. Logging and Debugging Best Practices

- Use Python's built-in logging module or a library like loguru for structured logs.

- In production, turn **debug=False** and run behind a stable WSGI server (like Gunicorn or uWSGI).

- For advanced debugging in local development, consider **Flask DebugToolbar** or pdb.

5. Connecting Your Front-End to Python APIs

5.1. Fetching Data with JavaScript (Fetch API, Axios, etc.)

On the client side, you can use:

1. **JavaScript's Fetch API**:

javascript

```javascript
fetch('/api/users')
  .then(response => response.json())
  .then(data => {
    console.log(data);
  })
  .catch(err => console.error(err));
```

2. **Axios**:

javascript

```javascript
axios.get('/api/users')
  .then(response => {
    console.log(response.data);
  })
  .catch(error => console.error(error));
```

Either approach handles asynchronous requests seamlessly, returning a **Promise**. The front-end can parse the JSON payload and update the DOM or React/Vue state accordingly.

5.2. Handling CORS and Security Implications

If your front-end is served from a different domain (say, http://localhost:3000 for React while Flask runs on http://localhost:5000), you'll need to handle **Cross-Origin Resource Sharing (CORS)**. Flask provides the flask-cors extension:

```python

from flask_cors import CORS


app = Flask(__name__)
CORS(app)
```

This sets HTTP response headers like Access-Control-Allow-Origin: *. In a real production environment, you may restrict origins to trusted domains.

5.3. Displaying API Responses Dynamically in the Browser

Once you have the data, you can insert it into the DOM:

```javascript
```

```
fetch('/api/users')
  .then(res => res.json())
  .then(data => {
    const userList =
document.getElementById('userList');
    data.users.forEach(user => {
      const li = document.createElement('li');
      li.textContent = `${user.id} -
${user.name}`;
      userList.appendChild(li);
    });
  });
```

Or in a React component, store the data in state:

jsx

```
function UserList() {
  const [users, setUsers] = React.useState([]);

  React.useEffect(() => {
    fetch('/api/users')
      .then(res => res.json())
      .then(data => setUsers(data.users));
  }, []);
```

```
return (
  <ul>
    {users.map(u => <li
key={u.id}>{u.name}</li>)}
  </ul>
);
}
```

5.4. Error Handling in the Front-End

What if the server is down or returns an error? Your client code should handle such cases gracefully:

javascript

```
fetch('/api/users')
  .then(res => {
    if (!res.ok) throw new Error('Network response
was not ok ' + res.status);
    return res.json();
  })
  .then(data => {
    // Update UI
  })
  .catch(err => {
    // Show error message or fallback
    console.error('Fetch failed:', err);
```

```
});
```

This ensures you don't break the UI if the server experiences issues.

---

6. Real-World Example: Creating a Python API to Fetch User Data and Display It on a Webpage

6.1. Project Overview and Requirements

We'll build a small user-management system:

- **Endpoints:**

    - GET /api/users returns all users.

    - GET /api/users/<id> returns details for a specific user.

    - POST /api/users adds a new user.

    - (Optional) PUT or DELETE for editing or removing users.

- **Front-End:**

    - A simple HTML page that fetches user data from our Flask API.

    - Displays user info in a list.

6.2. Setting Up the Flask Application

Create app.py:

python

```python
from flask import Flask, request, jsonify
from flask_cors import CORS

app = Flask(__name__)
CORS(app)

# In-memory data store for demonstration
USERS = [
```

```python
    {"id": 1, "name": "Alice", "email":
"alice@example.com"},
    {"id": 2, "name": "Bob", "email":
"bob@example.com"},
]


@app.route('/api/users', methods=['GET'])
def get_users():
    return jsonify({"users": USERS}), 200


@app.route('/api/users/<int:user_id>',
methods=['GET'])
def get_user(user_id):
    user = next((u for u in USERS if u['id'] ==
user_id), None)
    if user:
        return jsonify(user), 200
    return jsonify({"error": "User not found"}),
404


@app.route('/api/users', methods=['POST'])
def create_user():
    data = request.get_json()
    if not data or 'name' not in data or 'email'
not in data:
```

```python
        return jsonify({"error": "Invalid
request"}), 400


    new_id = max(u['id'] for u in USERS) + 1 if
USERS else 1
    new_user = {
        "id": new_id,
        "name": data['name'],
        "email": data['email']
    }
    USERS.append(new_user)
    return jsonify(new_user), 201


if __name__ == '__main__':
    app.run(debug=True)
```

Key Points:

- CORS(app) allows cross-origin requests from any domain.

- We store user data in an **in-memory list** USERS for simplicity. In production, you'd use a database.

- request.get_json() parses JSON from the request body.

- We generate a new **ID** by taking the max current **ID** plus one.

6.3. Implementing the "User" Model and In-Memory Storage

Right now, we have a dictionary for each user. This is fine for demos, but in real code, you might:

- Create a User class with fields and methods.

- Integrate an ORM like SQLAlchemy and a relational database.

- Or use a NoSQL approach like MongoDB with a library such as PyMongo.

6.4. Defining Endpoints for Fetching User Data

We already have:

- GET /api/users returns all users.

- GET /api/users/<int:user_id> fetches a single user by ID.

- POST /api/users to create a new user.

Optionally, we could add:

python

```
@app.route('/api/users/<int:user_id>',
methods=['PUT'])
```

```python
def update_user(user_id):
    data = request.get_json()
    user = next((u for u in USERS if u['id'] ==
user_id), None)
    if not user:
        return jsonify({"error": "User not
found"}), 404

    # Update fields if provided
    if 'name' in data:
        user['name'] = data['name']
    if 'email' in data:
        user['email'] = data['email']

    return jsonify(user), 200

@app.route('/api/users/<int:user_id>',
methods=['DELETE'])
def delete_user(user_id):
    global USERS
    original_length = len(USERS)
    USERS = [u for u in USERS if u['id'] !=
user_id]
    if len(USERS) == original_length:
        return jsonify({"error": "User not
found"}), 404
```

```
    return jsonify({"message": "User deleted"}),
200
```

6.5. Building a Minimal Front-End to Consume the API

Create an index.html:

```
html
```

```html
<!DOCTYPE html>
<html>
<head>
  <meta charset="UTF-8" />
  <title>User Management</title>
</head>
<body>
  <h1>User Management</h1>
  <div>
    <ul id="userList"></ul>
  </div>

  <h2>Add a New User</h2>
  <div>
    <input type="text" id="nameInput"
placeholder="Name" />
```

```
    <input type="text" id="emailInput"
placeholder="Email" />
    <button id="addUserBtn">Add User</button>
  </div>

  <script>
    const userList =
document.getElementById('userList');
    const nameInput =
document.getElementById('nameInput');
    const emailInput =
document.getElementById('emailInput');
    const addUserBtn =
document.getElementById('addUserBtn');

    function fetchUsers() {
      fetch('http://127.0.0.1:5000/api/users')
        .then(res => res.json())
        .then(data => {
          userList.innerHTML = '';
          data.users.forEach(user => {
            const li =
document.createElement('li');
            li.textContent = `${user.id} -
${user.name} (${user.email})`;
            userList.appendChild(li);
```

```
      });
    })
    .catch(err => console.error('Failed to
fetch users:', err));
  }


  function addUser() {
    const name = nameInput.value.trim();
    const email = emailInput.value.trim();
    if (!name || !email) return alert('Please
enter valid name and email');

    fetch('http://127.0.0.1:5000/api/users', {
      method: 'POST',
      headers: {
        'Content-Type': 'application/json'
      },
      body: JSON.stringify({ name, email })
    })
    .then(res => res.json())
    .then(newUser => {
      console.log('User created:', newUser);
      fetchUsers(); // refresh the list
      nameInput.value = '';
      emailInput.value = '';
    })
```

```
      .catch(err => console.error('Error creating
user:', err));
    }


    // Initial load
    fetchUsers();


    // Button click
    addUserBtn.addEventListener('click', addUser);
  </script>
</body>
</html>
```

Explanation:

1. We define a fetchUsers() function to GET /api/users and then display them in an unordered list.

2. We define an addUser() function to do a POST /api/users with the user's name and email in JSON format.

3. On load, fetchUsers() populates the list.

4. Clicking **Add User** triggers addUser(), which, upon success, calls fetchUsers() again.

6.6. Testing the Integration and Debugging

1. **Run** your Flask app with python app.py.

2. **Open** index.html in your browser (or serve it from a local dev server).

3. **Check** the JavaScript console for any errors.

4. **Add** a user via the input fields. The new user should appear in the list if everything is set up correctly.

5. If you face **CORS** errors, ensure Flask-CORS is installed and configured.

6. Use **network dev tools** to verify the requests and responses are as expected.

6.7. Potential Enhancements (Authentication, Databases, etc.)

- **Authentication**: Use JSON Web Tokens (JWT) or session-based auth to secure your endpoints.

- **Database Integration**: Replace the in-memory list with a real database.

- **Pagination**: If the user list is huge, add query params like ?page=2 or ?limit=10 to optimize data transfer.

- **Complex Front-End**: A React or Vue interface for a smoother user experience, complete with routing and form validation.

7. Deployment Considerations

7.1. Choosing a Production Server (Gunicorn, uWSGI, etc.)

Flask's built-in server is for development only. For production:

1. **Gunicorn**: A popular Python WSGI HTTP server; easy to set up.

2. **uWSGI**: Another robust option.

3. **Nginx** or **Apache** can reverse-proxy to your Flask process for better performance, SSL termination, etc.

7.2. Containerization with Docker

To ensure consistency:

1. Create a Dockerfile that installs Python, sets up your virtual environment, and runs your Flask app.

2. Optionally, define a docker-compose.yml to handle the entire stack, including databases.

3. Deploy the image to a cloud service or on-prem infrastructure for easy scaling and versioning.

7.3. Cloud Hosting and Scalability (AWS, Heroku, DigitalOcean)

Whether you use:

- **AWS Elastic Beanstalk** or **EC2**

- **Heroku** (which detects Python apps via requirements.txt)

- **DigitalOcean** (Docker droplets or managed app platform)

...it's generally straightforward to deploy your Flask API if you're mindful of environment variables, logging, and the underlying server environment.

7.4. CI/CD for Flask APIs

Automate building, testing, and deploying:

- Integrate with GitHub Actions or GitLab CI.

- Run unit tests, lint checks, and security scans on each commit.

- If successful, push the final image or code to your hosting platform.

8. Security and Best Practices

8.1. Authentication and Authorization (JWT, OAuth)

To secure your API:

1. **JWT**: Clients send an access token in the Authorization header.

2. **OAuth**: For more complex scenarios or 3rd-party integrations, OAuth flows can protect resources.

3. **Session Tokens**: Traditional for server-side sessions, though less common in purely stateless REST APIs.

8.2. HTTPS Everywhere and SSL Certificates

Always serve your API over **HTTPS**:

- For local dev, use a self-signed certificate or tools like mkcert.

- For production, get a certificate from Let's Encrypt, or rely on your cloud platform's managed SSL solutions.

8.3. Rate Limiting and Throttling

If your service might receive heavy or malicious traffic, implement:

- **Flask-Limiter** or custom logic to track IP-based request counts.

- Caching layers or specialized proxies (e.g., **Cloudflare**) that can throttle abusive IPs.

8.4. Input Validation and Sanitization

Even though your API might only accept JSON, never trust client input:

- Validate request data thoroughly.

- Use Python libraries like **Pydantic** or **Marshmallow** to define schemas.

- Filter out suspicious input or run checks for injection attempts if your code interacts with a database.

---

9. Performance Tuning

9.1. Using Caching for Frequent Requests

If certain endpoints are queried often (e.g., a user list), consider caching:

- **In-memory**: Tools like **Flask-Caching** with a simple dictionary store.

- **Redis** or **Memcached**: Distribute caching across multiple servers for higher scalability.

9.2. Profiling Flask Endpoints

Check where your code might slow down:

- The built-in cProfile library or the flask-profiler extension can reveal bottlenecks.

- Optimize database queries, reduce external service calls, or consider asynchronous patterns if you have CPU-bound tasks.

9.3. Async Python APIs (Flask vs. FastAPI)

While Flask 2.0 introduced some asynchronous capabilities, if you need high concurrency and truly async endpoints, you might evaluate **FastAPI**, a newer Python framework designed around async/await. However, Flask remains perfectly adequate for a wide range of typical API workloads, especially if you scale horizontally with multiple worker processes.

10. Conclusion

Flask's simplicity and flexibility make it a top choice for quickly spinning up **RESTful APIs** in Python. From a few lines of code to fully production-ready services with advanced authentication, logging, and scaling strategies, Flask grows with your application's needs. By structuring your routes thoughtfully, returning consistent JSON responses, and adhering to best practices like environment-based configurations and secure coding, you'll create APIs that are both robust and easy for front-end clients to consume.

We covered:

1. **API fundamentals** and how they enable modern app architectures.

2. **Setting up Flask** for essential routes, including JSON responses, HTTP methods, and status codes.

3. **Structuring your project** with blueprints and config management for maintainability.

4. **Connecting front-ends** with JavaScript to retrieve data from Flask endpoints and display it seamlessly to users.

5. **A real-world example** demonstrating user management, from GET and POST endpoints in Flask to a front-end that fetches and updates data dynamically.

6. **Deployment strategies**, **security** measures, and **performance** tips for scaling your Flask API.

With these insights, you can confidently build and integrate a Python-based API for virtually any scenario—from small personal projects to enterprise-scale microservices. As you continue to explore advanced topics like caching, asynchronous patterns, or bridging authentication frameworks, you'll find that Flask's ecosystem and minimalistic design keep you firmly in control of your codebase, ensuring you deliver fast, secure, and maintainable services to your users.

Chapter 13: JavaScript Advanced Topics: Promises and Asynchronous Programming

---

1. Introduction to Asynchronous JavaScript

JavaScript is often described as a **single-threaded** language. In simpler terms, it means that JavaScript processes tasks one at a time, in sequence. However, modern web applications constantly perform multiple operations that might take variable time to complete—like fetching data from a server or reading files from a device. If these tasks were purely **synchronous**, the entire page could freeze while waiting, making for a terrible user experience.

Asynchronous programming in JavaScript solves this problem, allowing tasks to occur **in parallel** with user interactions. As soon as an asynchronous function is invoked, JavaScript can continue running other code. When the operation completes, JavaScript fires a callback or resolves a **promise** to let you know the result is ready.

In this chapter, we'll dive deep into the advanced topics of **Promises**, **async/await**, and the underlying **event loop**. You'll learn how these tools provide clean, intuitive ways to handle tasks such as data fetching, dynamic UI rendering, and real-time updates, all without blocking the main thread. Finally, we'll put it all into practice by building a real-world example: a dynamic content-loading app that ensures the UI remains responsive while data is fetched asynchronously.

---

2. What Are Promises?

A **promise** in JavaScript is a special object that links an asynchronous operation's **producing code** (the code that actually does something, like an HTTP request) to the **consuming code** (the code that needs to do something after the operation completes). Promises replaced callback-based patterns as the primary way to handle async flows because they provide more clarity, error-handling capabilities, and chainable composition.

2.1. The Evolution from Callbacks to Promises

Historically, JavaScript used **callbacks**:

js

```js
fetchData('https://api.example.com/data', function
(err, data) {
  if (err) {
    // Handle error
  } else {
    // Use data
  }
});
```

While callbacks work, they can lead to **"callback hell"** when multiple operations depend on each other. Callbacks also complicate error handling—if something fails, you either pass the error along or handle it within nested callbacks.

Promises simplify this:

```
js
```

```js
fetch('https://api.example.com/data')
  .then(response => {
    // parse response
  })
  .catch(err => {
    // handle error
  });
```

Each .then returns a **new** promise, allowing you to chain them. Errors automatically propagate through the chain to the nearest .catch.

2.2. Core Promise States and Methods (then, catch, finally)

A promise can be in one of three states:

1. **Pending**: The operation has started, but not finished.

2. **Fulfilled**: The operation completed successfully; the promise has a resolved value.

3. **Rejected**: The operation failed; the promise has a reason for rejection (often an error object).

Promises have methods to react to these states:

- **.then(onFulfilled, onRejected?)**: Called when the promise is fulfilled (and optionally if it's rejected, though usually you use .catch).

- **.catch(onRejected)**: Captures any errors from the promise chain.

- **.finally(onFinally)**: Runs regardless of success or failure. Often used for cleanup or toggling UI states (e.g., turning off a loading spinner).

For example:

js

```js
doAsyncWork()
  .then(result => {
    console.log('Work done:', result);
  })
  .catch(error => {
    console.error('Something went wrong:', error);
  })
  .finally(() => {
    console.log('Async task completed (success or
error).');
  });
```

2.3. Chaining Promises for Complex Workflows

Because .then returns a promise, you can chain multiple .thens to handle sequential tasks:

js

```js
fetch('https://api.example.com/user/123')
```

```
.then(response => response.json())
.then(user => {
  // Use user data
  return
fetch(`https://api.example.com/orders/${user.id}`)
;
})
.then(response => response.json())
.then(orders => {
  console.log('User orders:', orders);
})
.catch(err => console.error('Error:', err));
```

This is more readable than nested callbacks. Each step can return data for the next step.

2.4. Error Handling Patterns with Promises

Errors propagate until caught:

js

```
fetchData()
  .then(parseData)
  .then(saveData)
  .then(showSuccessMessage)
  .catch(err => {
    // Catches errors from *any* previous step
```

```
    console.error('Error in chain:', err);
  });
```

If parseData or saveData fails, the .catch at the end sees the error. For partial or fallback logic, you might handle errors at multiple points:

js

```js
fetchConfig()
  .then(config => doSomething(config))
  .catch(err => {
    // handle only config errors
    return defaultConfig;
  })
  .then(result => {
    // next step
  })
  .catch(err => {
    // final catch for any leftover errors
  });
```

3. Async/Await: The Next Level of Asynchronous Code

Async/await is built on top of promises, but it offers a more synchronous-looking style. This approach can make complex asynchronous code easier to read and maintain.

3.1. Understanding Async Functions

Mark a function async:

```
js
```

```js
async function fetchData() {
  return 'Hello';
}
```

An async function always returns a **promise**. When you call fetchData(), you get a promise that eventually resolves to 'Hello'. If the function throws an error, the promise rejects.

3.2. Awaiting Promises and Error Handling with try/catch

Inside an async function, you can use the await keyword on any promise:

```
js
```

```
async function loadUser(userId) {
  try {
    const response = await
fetch(`https://api.example.com/users/${userId}`);
    if (!response.ok) {
      throw new Error(`Failed to load user:
${response.status}`);
    }
    const user = await response.json();
    return user;
  } catch (error) {
    console.error('Error loading user:', error);
    throw error; // re-throw if you want to handle
it elsewhere
  }
}
```

This code looks synchronous, but under the hood, it's non-blocking. The function execution pauses at await until the promise resolves, then continues.

3.3. Combining Multiple Async Calls in Sequential or Parallel Flows

Sequential: Each step depends on the previous:

js

```js
async function loadUserAndOrders(userId) {
  const userResponse = await
fetch(`/user/${userId}`);
  const user = await userResponse.json();
  const ordersResponse = await
fetch(`/orders/${user.id}`);
  const orders = await ordersResponse.json();
  return { user, orders };
}
```

Parallel: Fire multiple requests simultaneously:

js

```js
async function loadDataInParallel() {
  const [users, products] = await Promise.all([
    fetch('/api/users').then(res => res.json()),
    fetch('/api/products').then(res => res.json())
  ]);
  return { users, products };
}
```

Promise.all waits for all promises to resolve or for one to reject. The advantage is performance: two or more operations run at once rather than in sequence.

3.4. The Role of Promise.all, Promise.race, and Other Combinators

- **Promise.all()**: Resolves when **all** promises in the array resolve (or rejects if any reject).

- **Promise.race()**: Resolves/rejects as soon as **one** of the promises resolves/rejects.

- **Promise.any()**: Resolves as soon as **one** promise resolves, but only rejects if all fail.

- **Promise.allSettled()**: Waits for all to finish, returning an array describing each promise's outcome (fulfilled or rejected).

These combinators let you orchestrate complex async flows. For instance, you could use Promise.race() to implement a timeout: if an operation takes too long, you race it against a promise that rejects after a certain delay.

4. Event Loop and Concurrency

4.1. JavaScript's Single-Threaded Nature

Despite dealing with asynchronous tasks, JavaScript still runs on a single thread: there's one **call stack** that processes instructions. So how does it handle parallel tasks like network I/O or timers?

4.2. The Event Loop Explained (Call Stack, Callback Queue, Microtasks)

When an async operation (like a fetch) finishes, its callback or promise resolution doesn't immediately run. Instead, it gets queued in the **microtask queue** (for promise callbacks) or the **callback queue** (for DOM events, setTimeout, etc.). Once the call stack is empty, the event loop checks the microtask queue first, then the callback queue. If any tasks are in these queues, they move onto the call stack and execute.

4.3. Microtasks vs. Macrotasks: Where Promises Fit In

- **Microtasks**: Promises use microtasks. After each run of the main code block, microtasks run **before** the next rendering or callback.

- **Macrotasks:** Timers (setTimeout), DOM events, or message events. They typically occur after microtasks finish.

This is why promise callbacks can run **before** a setTimeout(..., 0) callback, even if both were triggered at roughly the same time.

4.4. Performance Implications and Best Practices

- Keep asynchronous tasks short if they run in microtasks, to avoid blocking subsequent tasks.

- Avoid deep nested loops or synchronous computations in promise callbacks, or the UI can still appear frozen.

- Profile your code if you suspect heavy computations are blocking the event loop.

---

5. Real-World Example: Creating an App that Loads Content Dynamically Without Blocking the UI

5.1. Project Overview and Goals

We'll build a simple **"Dynamic News"** page that fetches articles from a mock API. Requirements:

1. **Display** a list of articles upon page load.

2. **Show** a loading spinner while data is being fetched, so the UI remains responsive.

3. **Handle** errors gracefully (e.g., network offline, server down).

4. **Optionally** let users click a button to fetch more articles or filter existing ones.

The final result: No matter how long the fetch takes, the user can still click buttons or scroll the page without locking the main thread.

5.2. Setting Up the HTML and Basic Styles

Create index.html:

html

```html
<!DOCTYPE html>
<html lang="en">
<head>
  <meta charset="UTF-8">
  <title>Dynamic News</title>
  <link rel="stylesheet" href="styles.css">
</head>
<body>
  <h1>Latest News</h1>
  <div id="loading" class="hidden">Loading...</div>
  <ul id="articleList"></ul>
  <button id="loadMoreBtn">Load More Articles</button>

  <script src="app.js"></script>
</body>
</html>
```

styles.css might have:

```css
body {
  font-family: Arial, sans-serif;
  margin: 20px;
}


.hidden {
  display: none;
}


#loading {
  color: #555;
  margin-bottom: 1em;
}


#articleList li {
  border-bottom: 1px solid #ccc;
  padding: 10px 0;
}
```

We set #loading to .hidden by default to keep it invisible until a fetch is in progress.

5.3. Writing the JavaScript with Promises or Async/Await

app.js:

js

```
const loadingEl =
document.getElementById('loading');
const articleList =
document.getElementById('articleList');
const loadMoreBtn =
document.getElementById('loadMoreBtn');

let page = 1; // track pagination or offset

async function fetchArticles(page) {
  // Display the loading indicator
  loadingEl.classList.remove('hidden');

  try {
    const response = await
fetch(`https://api.example.com/news?page=${page}`)
;
    if (!response.ok) {
      throw new Error(`Server error:
${response.status}`);
```

```javascript
    }
    const data = await response.json();
    // Assume data.articles is an array of article
objects
    return data.articles;
  } catch (error) {
    console.error('Error fetching articles:',
error);
    alert('Failed to load articles. Please try
again.');
    return [];
  } finally {
    // Hide the loading indicator
    loadingEl.classList.add('hidden');
  }
}


async function loadArticles() {
  const articles = await fetchArticles(page);
  articles.forEach(article => {
    const li = document.createElement('li');
    li.innerHTML = `
      <h2>${article.title}</h2>
      <p>${article.summary}</p>
    `;
    articleList.appendChild(li);
```

```
   });
   page += 1; // increment for next batch
}
```

```
// On page load, load the first set of articles
loadArticles();
```

```
loadMoreBtn.addEventListener('click',
loadArticles);
```

Explanation:

1. We have a **global** page variable to handle pagination.

2. fetchArticles is **async** and returns an array of articles or an empty array if something fails.

3. We show the loading element at the start, and remove it once the fetch is done (in a finally block).

4. In loadArticles, we call fetchArticles and then create <li> elements for each article.

5. The user can click "Load More Articles" to fetch the next page.

5.4. Handling Errors and Timeouts Gracefully

To address timeouts:

js

```js
function fetchWithTimeout(url, options, timeout =
5000) {
  return new Promise((resolve, reject) => {
    const controller = new AbortController();
    const signal = controller.signal;

    const timer = setTimeout(() => {
      controller.abort();
      reject(new Error('Request timed out'));
    }, timeout);

    fetch(url, { ...options, signal })
      .then(response => {
        clearTimeout(timer);
        resolve(response);
      })
      .catch(err => {
        clearTimeout(timer);
        reject(err);
      });
  });
```

```
}
Now in fetchArticles:
js


async function fetchArticles(page) {
  // ...
  const response = await
fetchWithTimeout(`https://api.example.com/news?pag
e=${page}`, {}, 5000);
  // ...
}
```

If the server doesn't respond in 5 seconds, we gracefully handle the error.

5.5. Optimizing for Performance

- **Pagination** reduces the amount of data fetched at once.

- We only manipulate the DOM once per article. If performance becomes an issue, consider **document fragments** or templating libraries.

- For heavy operations (like sorting or processing large data sets) after fetch, do it in a **Web Worker** to keep the UI responsive.

6. Practical Patterns and Tips

6.1. Canceling or Aborting Async Operations

Using AbortController (as shown above) is a neat way to **cancel** a fetch. For other async tasks, you might track a "canceled" flag or use external libraries that support cancellation.

6.2. Throttling and Debouncing Repetitive Calls

If a user types into a search box, you don't want to fetch results on **every** keystroke. **Throttle** or **debounce** can rate-limit those calls:

js

```js
function debounce(fn, delay) {
  let timer;
  return (...args) => {
    clearTimeout(timer);
    timer = setTimeout(() => fn(...args), delay);
  };
}
```

6.3. Using Generators for Advanced Async Patterns (Brief Overview)

Generators (function*) plus a runner function can mimic async flows. This was a stepping stone before async/await. Most new code uses async/await instead, but you might still see generator-based code in older projects or advanced libraries.

6.4. Using Modules and Build Tools with Async Code

If your codebase grows, you'll likely adopt ES modules (import/export) and bundlers like **Webpack**, **Rollup**, or **Parcel**. Async/await may need transpilation for older browsers. Tools like Babel handle this automatically.

---

7. Testing and Debugging Asynchronous Code

7.1. Tools for Logging and Monitoring

1. **Console logs**: Print relevant data or error messages in promise chains or try/catch blocks.

2. **Network logs**: In devtools, watch the timeline of requests.

3. **Monitoring**: In production, track logs or metrics via services like Logstash, Kibana, or a cloud provider's tools.

7.2. Using DevTools to Trace Async Calls

Chrome or Firefox devtools let you step through promise-based code, set breakpoints in .then() callbacks, or observe stack traces for rejections. Also, they highlight unhandled promise rejections if you forget to catch an error.

7.3. Testing Promises with Jest, Mocha, or Cypress

In Jest:

js

```js
test('fetches data correctly', async () => {
  const data = await fetchDataMock();
  expect(data).toEqual(expectedData);
});
```

If you use .then, you might do return fetchDataMock().then(...) so Jest knows to wait for the promise. Alternatively, use the built-in async test:

js

```js
test('async test example', async () => {
  const response = await fetch('...');
  expect(response.ok).toBe(true);
```

```
});
```

7.4. Common Pitfalls (Memory Leaks, Lost Promises, Unhandled Rejections)

- **Memory leaks**: If you store references to resolved promises or keep intervals running after the component unmounts (in frameworks like React), you can have stale data or memory overhead.

- **Lost promises**: If you never .catch an error, in Node.js or new browser versions, you might see an "Unhandled Promise Rejection" warning.

- **Infinite loops**: If a .then or async function re-calls itself inadvertently, you can crash the event loop.

---

8. Next Steps and Future Trends

8.1. Server-Side JavaScript and Async Patterns in Node.js

The same promise/async code you've learned applies to Node.js back ends. Node uses an event-driven architecture, so you can handle file I/O, network requests, and database calls using async/await or streams. Tools like **Koa**, **Express**, or **Fastify** rely heavily on asynchronous code to serve high-traffic APIs.

8.2. Web Workers for Parallelism

While JavaScript is single-threaded, **Web Workers** let you run code in separate background threads. This is crucial for CPU-intensive tasks like image processing or data crunching without blocking the main UI.

8.3. The Ongoing Evolution of Async Patterns

JavaScript's concurrency model continues to evolve:

- **Top-Level Await**: In ES2022, modules can use await at the top level, simplifying some patterns.

- **Temporal Dead Zone** in asynchronous context is an area of exploration.

- **Suspense** in frameworks like React uses concurrency features to manage asynchronous data rendering.

---

9. Conclusion

Asynchronous programming is a **cornerstone** of modern JavaScript development. Understanding **promises**, **async/await**, and the **event**

loop is key to writing responsive, efficient code that handles real-world tasks like fetching data, reading files, or performing long-running operations without blocking the UI.

- **Promises** improved upon callbacks by centralizing error handling, enabling chaining, and reducing nesting.

- **Async/await** offers a cleaner, more synchronous style for reading asynchronous flows, making code more maintainable and debug-friendly.

- The **event loop** and concurrency model ensure JavaScript's single thread can juggle multiple tasks effectively.

- By combining these techniques with good patterns like Promise.all, microtask awareness, and robust testing, you'll build reliable apps that deliver seamless user experiences—even under heavy data fetching or complex logic.

In the **dynamic content loading** example we built, we saw how to show a loading indicator, retrieve data from a server, and populate the UI non-blockingly—all while allowing the user to continue interacting with the page. This is the practical essence of asynchronous programming: letting your app remain fluid and interactive as tasks complete in the background.

Armed with these insights, you can confidently tackle more advanced patterns—like streaming responses, concurrency management, or parallel computing in the browser—and push your JavaScript code to new heights of scalability and performance.

Chapter 14: Security Best Practices in Front-End Development

1. Introduction: Why Security Matters

Front-end developers often focus on **user experience**, **layout**, and **performance**—but **security** is equally vital. A single vulnerability can compromise user data, ruin an organization's reputation, and lead to legal ramifications. While back-end systems traditionally handle core logic and data storage, front-end code still holds sensitive information (tokens, user details) and interacts with third-party services that could expose attack surfaces.

Modern web applications operate in an interconnected ecosystem, with the **browser** handling everything from storing session tokens to rendering dynamic JavaScript libraries. If attackers can exploit a front-end flaw—like injecting malicious scripts or stealing tokens—they can escalate to more devastating attacks, such as taking over accounts or exfiltrating user data.

By embracing **secure coding practices** from the start—validating data, sanitizing outputs, hardening authentication, and more—you fortify your application against common threats. This chapter explores the top security risks facing front-end developers today, including **Cross-Site Scripting (XSS)**, authentication pitfalls, session management, and offers a real-world example of building a **secure login page**. Additionally, we'll survey advanced measures like **Content Security Policy (CSP)**, Subresource Integrity (SRI), and best practices for testing and maintaining your application's security posture in an ever-evolving threat landscape.

2. Common Threats in Front-End Environments

2.1. Cross-Site Scripting (XSS)

One of the most pervasive client-side vulnerabilities, **XSS** allows malicious scripts to run within the user's browser. Attackers might inject scripts via unsanitized user inputs or tampered URLs. Once injected, these scripts can steal cookies, impersonate users, or redirect them to phishing sites.

2.2. Cross-Site Request Forgery (CSRF)

CSRF exploits the fact that browsers automatically include session cookies when making requests. An attacker tricks a logged-in user into making unwanted requests—for example, forcing them to submit a malicious form or trigger an API call that changes account settings.

2.3. SQL Injection and API Vulnerabilities

While **SQL Injection** typically occurs on the server side, front-end code can inadvertently pass harmful queries if it fails to properly sanitize or validate inputs. If your API is not robustly validating the data, injection vulnerabilities can slip through.

2.4. Man-in-the-Middle Attacks

In the absence of **HTTPS/TLS**, attackers can intercept traffic between the user's browser and the server, reading or modifying data in transit. This is especially dangerous for login credentials or sensitive data.

---

3. Principles of Secure Front-End Development

3.1. The Principle of Least Privilege

Always provide the **minimum level of access** necessary. Don't give your front-end unlimited capabilities—like exposing advanced admin endpoints or including sensitive tokens in the client—unless absolutely required.

3.2. Defense in Depth

No single measure is foolproof. Layer multiple protections—**input validation, CSP, token-based authentication**—so if one layer fails, another can catch the threat.

3.3. "Never Trust User Input"

Even if you believe some data is safe, treat it as untrusted by default. Always sanitize or escape potentially malicious characters, and never assume user-provided content is free of scripts or exploits.

3.4. Shifting Left: Early Security Testing

Involve security considerations from the start of your development lifecycle. Running vulnerability scans and code audits once the project is "finished" can be too late or more expensive to fix.

4. Cross-Site Scripting (XSS): How to Avoid Malicious Scripts

4.1. Types of XSS (Stored, Reflected, DOM-based)

1. **Stored XSS**: The malicious script is permanently stored on the server (e.g., in a database) and served to users.

2. **Reflected XSS**: The script is part of a request or URL and is "reflected" back by the server. Attackers trick users into clicking malicious links.

3. **DOM-based XSS**: The vulnerability resides in client-side JavaScript that modifies the DOM without proper sanitization.

4.2. Sanitizing and Escaping User-Provided Content

Use well-maintained libraries or frameworks to **sanitize** content. For instance, in React, by default:

```jsx

<div>{userInput}</div>
```

Is safe because React escapes strings. But if you use **dangerouslySetInnerHTML**, you must manually sanitize. Outside frameworks, you might rely on libraries like DOMPurify or sanitize-html.

4.3. Setting Content Security Policy (CSP)

A **Content Security Policy** helps the browser prevent XSS by restricting the sources of scripts, styles, and other resources. For example:

```csharp
Content-Security-Policy:
  default-src 'self';
  script-src 'self';
  object-src 'none';
```

This reduces the risk of inline script execution or loading scripts from untrusted domains. CSP can also block mixed content or prompt you to enable strict dynamic loading rules.

4.4. Framework Tools and Best Practices (React, Vue, Angular)

- **React**: Avoid dangerouslySetInnerHTML; rely on built-in escaping. If absolutely necessary, sanitize thoroughly.

- **Vue**: Use template expressions ({{ data }}) or directives that automatically escape HTML. Beware of v-html.

- **Angular**: Angular's templating automatically sanitizes expressions. For bypassing that, you must explicitly call DomSanitizer, which is risky.

4.5. Real-World XSS Examples and Lessons

From social media giants to e-commerce sites, XSS is frequently found when user comments or images are displayed without proper sanitization. One infamous example was MySpace's "Samy worm," which used stored XSS to replicate across millions of profiles.

---

5. Authentication and Session Management

5.1. Implementing Secure Logins

Login pages are prime targets for attacks. Key steps:

1. Use **HTTPS** to encrypt credentials.

2. Validate inputs (e.g., email format, password strength).

3. Limit login attempts or set a short lockout after multiple failures to prevent brute-force attacks.

4. Implement server-side checks for user existence, password hashing, and user status (active/inactive).

5.2. Cookies vs. Tokens (JWT)

Cookies can hold session IDs, which the server uses to track authenticated sessions. However, they can be vulnerable to XSS if not flagged as **HttpOnly. JWT tokens** stored in browser memory or localStorage can also be stolen via XSS. Consider these trade-offs:

- Cookies with HttpOnly and Secure flags often mitigate direct JavaScript access.

- JWTs are stateless and easy for single-page apps to handle, but you must guard them carefully.

5.3. Session Storage, Local Storage, and Security Implications

- **Local Storage**: Persists data even if the browser tab is closed. If an attacker runs malicious scripts, they can read localStorage.

- **Session Storage**: Lasts until the tab or window closes, somewhat safer but still vulnerable if an attacker can run scripts.

- **Cookies**: If not HttpOnly, scripts can read them.

No single approach is perfect. Choose based on your threat model, ensuring strong protection against XSS, or rely on short-lived tokens with frequent refresh cycles.

5.4. Handling Tokens, Refresh Tokens, and Expiration

To avoid indefinite access, tokens should expire. A short-lived **access token** plus a **refresh token** stored in a secure cookie can let users keep sessions active without risking exposure if an attacker obtains the token. Always check token expiry server-side and request a new token only through a secure channel.

5.5. Password Handling, Storage, and Policy

On the back end, use strong hashing algorithms like **bcrypt** or **Argon2**. From the front-end perspective:

- Enforce minimum password length or complexity.

- Provide feedback (strength meters) but never reveal details like how many characters are correct.

- Avoid storing plaintext passwords or even hashed ones on the client.

6. Real-World Example: Building a Secure Login Page

6.1. Project Overview

We'll create a basic **login flow** that demonstrates front-end validations, secure form submission, token handling, and session management at a high level. Our design:

1. A **login form** with email and password fields.

2. **Client-side validation** to check for empty fields or minimal password length.

3. Submission to a **mock server** endpoint that returns either an error or a success JSON with a token.

4. **Storing the token** in an HTTP-only cookie or a memory-based approach for demonstration.

5. Display a personalized greeting if logged in, along with a logout option.

6.2. Creating the Front-End Structure (HTML and CSS)

index.html:

```html
html
```

```html
<!DOCTYPE html>
<html lang="en">
<head>
  <meta charset="UTF-8">
  <title>Secure Login</title>
  <link rel="stylesheet" href="styles.css">
</head>
<body>
  <div class="login-container">
    <h1>Secure Login</h1>
    <div id="errorMessage" class="hidden"></div>
    <form id="loginForm">
```

```html
      <label for="email">Email</label>
      <input type="email" id="email" required />

      <label for="password">Password</label>
      <input type="password" id="password"
required minlength="8" />

      <button type="submit"
id="loginBtn">Login</button>
    </form>
    <div id="welcomeMessage" class="hidden">
      <p id="welcomeText"></p>
      <button id="logoutBtn">Logout</button>
    </div>
  </div>
  <script src="login.js"></script>
</body>
</html>
```

styles.css (a minimal example):

```css
css

body {
  font-family: Arial, sans-serif;
  margin: 0;
  padding: 0;
```

```css
  background: #f7f7f7;
}
.login-container {
  width: 300px;
  margin: 80px auto;
  background: #fff;
  padding: 20px;
  border-radius: 8px;
  box-shadow: 0 0 8px rgba(0,0,0,0.1);
}
.hidden {
  display: none;
}
#errorMessage {
  color: red;
  margin-bottom: 10px;
}
```

6.3. Implementing Client-Side Validation with JavaScript

login.js:

js

```js
const loginForm =
document.getElementById('loginForm');
```

```javascript
const emailInput =
document.getElementById('email');
const passwordInput =
document.getElementById('password');
const loginBtn =
document.getElementById('loginBtn');
const errorMessage =
document.getElementById('errorMessage');
const welcomeMessage =
document.getElementById('welcomeMessage');
const welcomeText =
document.getElementById('welcomeText');
const logoutBtn =
document.getElementById('logoutBtn');


function showError(message) {
  errorMessage.textContent = message;
  errorMessage.classList.remove('hidden');
}


function hideError() {
  errorMessage.classList.add('hidden');
  errorMessage.textContent = '';
}


async function loginUser(email, password) {
```

```
    // In a real app, always use HTTPS and secure
server
  try {
    const response = await
fetch('https://example.com/api/login', {
      method: 'POST',
      headers: { 'Content-Type':
'application/json' },
      // Could set credentials: 'include' if using
cookies
      body: JSON.stringify({ email, password })
    });

    if (!response.ok) {
      const errData = await response.json();
      throw new Error(errData.message || `Login
failed: ${response.status}`);
    }

    // For demonstration, let's say the server
returns { token: "JWT_TOKEN", user: { name: "John"
} }
    const data = await response.json();
    // store token securely (HttpOnly cookie on
server side or localStorage for demonstration)
    localStorage.setItem('authToken', data.token);
```

```javascript
    // display welcome
    welcomeText.textContent = `Welcome,
${data.user.name}!`;
    loginForm.classList.add('hidden');
    welcomeMessage.classList.remove('hidden');

  } catch (error) {
    showError(error.message);
  }
}


loginForm.addEventListener('submit', (e) => {
  e.preventDefault();
  hideError();
  const email = emailInput.value.trim();
  const password = passwordInput.value.trim();

  if (!email) {
    showError('Email is required');
    return;
  }
  if (!password) {
    showError('Password is required');
    return;
  }
```

```
  if (password.length < 8) {
    showError('Password must be at least 8
characters');
    return;
  }

  loginUser(email, password);
});


logoutBtn.addEventListener('click', () => {
  // Clear token
  localStorage.removeItem('authToken');
  welcomeMessage.classList.add('hidden');
  loginForm.classList.remove('hidden');
  emailInput.value = '';
  passwordInput.value = '';
});
```

Explanation:

1. **Client-side checks**: Ensure email and password fields are non-empty and password is at least 8 characters.

2. **loginUser**: A function using **async/await** to POST credentials to a (mock) server endpoint. If successful, store the token in localStorage for demonstration, then show a welcome message.

3. If the server responds with an error (bad credentials, server error), we show an error message.

4. **Logout:** Clears the token and toggles the UI back to the login form.

6.4. Integrating with a Back-End Auth API

In a real scenario, the back-end might set an **HttpOnly cookie** with the session token or JWT. The front-end code changes slightly to accommodate that approach. If your server returns 2xx with a JSON body containing user info, that's fine. But for secure token handling, rely on server-managed cookies with **HttpOnly** and **Secure** flags, preventing direct JavaScript access.

6.5. Storing Session Data Securely

Storing the token in localStorage is not recommended for production if you can avoid it, because malicious scripts can read it. A better approach is to have the server set an **HttpOnly** cookie:

```js
await fetch('/api/login', {
  method: 'POST',
  body: JSON.stringify({ ... }),
  credentials: 'include'
```

```
});
```

Then the server can manage the cookie's creation. The front-end never sees the raw token, so XSS can't easily steal it (but you still must protect from XSS anyway).

6.6. Logging Out and Session Expiration

- **Log Out:** Either delete the cookie on the server or instruct the client to discard the token.

- **Session Expiration:** The back-end can set short cookie lifetimes or use refresh tokens. On the front-end, you might detect 401 Unauthorized responses, prompting a re-login.

---

7. Additional Security Measures

7.1. Protecting Against CSRF

CSRF is mitigated by including a **nonce** or **CSRF token** in your forms or AJAX requests, ensuring the request originated from your site:

1. Generate a random token server-side.

2. Insert it into the HTML form as a hidden input or send it in a custom header with JavaScript.

3. The server verifies this token before processing the request.

7.2. Using HTTPS/TLS and HSTS

Always serve your site over **HTTPS** to encrypt traffic and prevent eavesdropping or tampering. **HSTS (HTTP Strict Transport Security)** instructs browsers to only connect over HTTPS, even if the user types http://.

7.3. Subresource Integrity (SRI) for External Scripts

If you load external scripts from a CDN:

html

```html
<script
  src="https://cdn.example.com/script.js"
  integrity="sha384-KyZXEAg3QhqLMpG8..."
  crossorigin="anonymous">
</script>
```

SRI ensures that if the script at that URL is tampered with, the browser blocks it. This protects against compromised CDNs or MITM attacks.

7.4. Avoiding Mixed Content Warnings

Don't load any resources (scripts, images, etc.) via **HTTP** on an **HTTPS** site. Browsers show warnings or block them entirely. Ensure all resources use https:// or relative protocols.

7.5. Handling Browser Autofill and Input Fields

Browsers often autofill saved credentials. This can be a convenience but also a risk if someone gains physical access to a user's device. Use autocomplete="off" or new-password for sensitive fields where needed, though modern browsers might ignore it for login forms to help users.

---

8. Security Testing and Tools

8.1. Static Application Security Testing (SAST)

Analyze your code for known security issues. Tools like **ESLint** with security plugins, **SonarQube**, or specialized scanners can detect common insecure patterns.

8.2. Dynamic Application Security Testing (DAST)

Tools like **OWASP ZAP** or **Burp Suite** scan a running web app for vulnerabilities, simulating real attacks. They look for XSS injection points, insecure cookies, or missing security headers.

8.3. Penetration Testing and Bug Bounties

For higher assurance, hire professional **pentesters** or start a **bug bounty program** to encourage ethical hackers to report vulnerabilities. This approach uncovers real-world exploits that automated scans might miss.

8.4. Automated Auditing Tools (e.g., OWASP ZAP, npm audit)

- **npm audit** checks for known vulnerabilities in your dependencies.

- **OWASP ZAP** intercepts requests/responses to find suspicious parameters or config weaknesses.

9. Performance vs. Security

9.1. Impact of CSP and Other Headers on Performance

A **strict** CSP can prevent certain inline scripts or data URIs, forcing you to load resources from known domains, which can be beneficial for caching. However, implementing CSP incorrectly might cause build-time or run-time friction. Evaluate your architecture to ensure minimal overhead.

9.2. Balancing Usability, Speed, and Safety

Excessive friction—like overly strict password rules or constant re-logins—may alienate users. Achieve a **balance**: short session timeouts for critical actions, a reasonable password policy, and multi-factor authentication for advanced security.

9.3. Building a Performance-Oriented Secure Pipeline

Secure code doesn't have to slow your site:

1. **Optimize** your build for minimal JavaScript.

2. Use **code splitting** and lazy loading.

3. Deploy strict security headers only after thorough testing so they don't break your app.

4. Profile your site to confirm encryption overhead or additional security checks don't hamper user experience.

---

10. Best Practices Checklist

10.1. Coding and Validation

- Sanitize and escape all user inputs.

- Avoid inline JavaScript or HTML injections.

- Use proven libraries for any cryptography or hashing.

10.2. Data Handling and Storage

- Never store sensitive data in plain text in localStorage or cookies.

- Use short-lived tokens and rotate them frequently.

- Carefully manage permission levels and access checks.

10.3. Infrastructure and Deployment

- Enforce HTTPS/TLS with HSTS.

- Set up robust error monitoring and logging.

- Keep your server and third-party dependencies updated.

10.4. Response to Vulnerabilities and Updates

- Have a plan for **responsible disclosure** if an external researcher finds a bug.

- Patch quickly, issue new build versions.

- Communicate with users about major security fixes.

---

11. Conclusion

Security in front-end development is no longer optional. Attackers are increasingly sophisticated, exploiting everything from weak input validation to stolen JWTs. By combining **strong coding practices**, **defensive frameworks**, **secure authentication strategies**, and **security testing**, you can significantly reduce your risk.

The key lessons:

1. **Cross-Site Scripting** (XSS) remains a top threat—sanitize outputs, set CSP, and avoid unsafe DOM manipulations.

2. **Authentication and Session Management** demand careful token handling, secure cookies, and consistent checks for token expiration.

3. **Real-World Example**: Building a secure login page shows how to integrate these ideas—client-side validation, secure form submission, storing tokens, and preventing unauthorized use.

4. **Additional Measures** like CSRF tokens, Subresource Integrity, and strict HTTPS usage further bolster your app's defenses.

5. **Testing Tools** (SAST, DAST, pen tests) and a well-defined response plan ensure you keep up with evolving threats.

Ultimately, security is an ongoing **process**, not a one-off project milestone. Continual education, code reviews, and adoption of new standards will help you stay ahead. By embedding security from the earliest stages of development, you protect both your users and your reputation, fostering trust and reliability in your front-end applications.

Chapter 15: Deploying and Maintaining Python-Powered Web Apps

---

1. Introduction: The Importance of Deployment and Maintenance

Deployment and maintenance are the final, but crucial, steps in creating a Python-powered web app. Many developers spend months perfecting their code, but if the deployment is handled poorly, the application can fail to meet users' expectations. Whether you're deploying a simple personal project or a business-critical app, a robust deployment and maintenance strategy ensures your app runs smoothly and securely in a production environment.

In this chapter, we will explore how to deploy Python-powered web apps to two of the most popular cloud platforms, **Heroku** and **DigitalOcean**, comparing both for ease of use and flexibility. We will also discuss **best practices for maintaining and scaling** your app, covering debugging, monitoring, performance optimization, and security to ensure your app is reliable and user-friendly in the long run.

---

2. What is Web Deployment?

2.1. Understanding the Web Hosting Landscape

When you develop a Python web app, you're usually developing it on your local machine using a local development environment (like Flask or Django's built-in server). However, for others to interact with your web app, it needs to be **hosted on a public server**. **Web deployment** is the process of transferring your web app from your local development environment to a production server where it can be accessed by users over the internet.

Web hosting involves several components:

1. **Web Server**: Software that handles incoming requests and serves your app. Popular web servers include **Apache**, **Nginx**, and **Gunicorn** (specifically for Python web apps).

2. **Database Server**: The place where your data is stored. Common databases include **PostgreSQL**, **MySQL**, and **SQLite** for lightweight projects.

3. **File Storage**: For managing static assets like images, videos, and files that your application uses.

4. **SSL/TLS**: For securing data transmission via HTTPS.

2.2. The Role of Web Servers and Databases

A **web server** processes client requests and returns appropriate content. When a user visits a website, the web server receives that request and routes it to the correct application logic or files.

A **database server** stores your data. For example, if you're building a social media platform, a database server would store user profiles, posts, messages, and other content. Your Python app will often interact with the database to create, retrieve, update, and delete data.

2.3. Deployment Pipeline Basics

Deploying a web application involves several steps:

- **Code build and packaging**: Preparing your app to run on the target platform (e.g., bundling dependencies, preparing configuration files).

- **Environment setup**: Setting up the necessary environment variables, servers, and databases.

- **Deployment**: Moving the code to a live server, ensuring everything runs as expected.

- **Post-deployment actions**: Testing, monitoring, and debugging once the application is live.

2.4. The Importance of Automated Deployments

Automated deployments enable you to push updates and changes to your live app quickly and efficiently, without risking human error. Using continuous integration/continuous deployment (CI/CD) tools ensures that every change made to your codebase is automatically tested and deployed to production in a controlled and repeatable manner.

---

3. Preparing Your Python Web App for Deployment

Before you deploy your Python web app, it's essential to ensure your application is production-ready. This involves:

3.1. Setting Up the Environment

1. **Choose the right Python version**: Ensure your local development environment matches the Python version used in production. It's a good practice to specify the Python version in a runtime.txt file (Heroku) or by using a virtual environment for consistency.

2. **Install dependencies**: Use pip freeze > requirements.txt to list your project's dependencies. This will allow you to install them easily on the server with pip install -r requirements.txt.

3. **Configure environment variables**: Store sensitive information (like API keys and database credentials) in environment variables. Do not hard-code these values in your application code.

3.2. Dependencies and Requirements: Managing with requirements.txt

The requirements.txt file lists all of the dependencies your Python app needs to run. To generate the file, use:

```bash
```

```bash
pip freeze > requirements.txt
```

Make sure this file is committed to version control so that the deployment environment can install the same dependencies with:

```bash
```

```bash
pip install -r requirements.txt
```

3.3. Configuring Your Web Application for Production

Your app might behave differently in a development environment compared to production. Here are a few things to consider:

- **Disable debugging**: Disable Flask or Django's debug mode when deploying to production. In Flask, you can set app.config['DEBUG'] = False.

- **Set up logging**: Ensure that your app logs errors and other critical events to track and debug production issues.

- **Security settings**: Enable HTTPS, use secure cookies, and sanitize user inputs to prevent common security vulnerabilities like XSS and CSRF.

3.4. Using Version Control for Deployment

Deploying from version control systems like **Git** helps ensure a clean and reproducible deployment. For example, pushing code to a Git repository (like **GitHub, GitLab,** or **Bitbucket**) allows you to integrate automated deployment tools and roll back changes when necessary.

4. Choosing a Hosting Platform: Heroku vs. DigitalOcean

4.1. Why Use Heroku for Python Web Apps?

Heroku is a **Platform as a Service (PaaS)** that makes deploying web applications incredibly easy. Some advantages of Heroku:

- **Easy Setup**: With just a few commands, you can deploy your Python web app.

- **Free Tier**: Heroku offers a free tier for small projects, making it a great choice for beginners or small-scale apps.

- **Managed Infrastructure**: Heroku abstracts much of the infrastructure management, allowing developers to focus on writing code rather than dealing with the complexities of configuring servers.

4.2. Why Use DigitalOcean for Python Web Apps?

DigitalOcean is an affordable cloud infrastructure provider, offering more control than PaaS options like Heroku. Some advantages of DigitalOcean:

- **Flexibility**: DigitalOcean provides Virtual Private Servers (called "Droplets") that give you full control over your server environment.

- **Cost-effective**: DigitalOcean is cheaper than many other cloud providers, and you can easily scale your app as needed.

- **Customizable Infrastructure**: If you need more customization or need to handle more complex setups, DigitalOcean is a great option.

4.3. Comparing Hosting Options: Ease of Use vs. Flexibility

- **Heroku** is easier to use but offers limited control over infrastructure.

- **DigitalOcean** offers more flexibility but requires more setup and configuration, especially for scaling and managing your app.

4.4. Setting Up Heroku for Python Deployment

1. Create a Heroku account at https://heroku.com.

2. Install the Heroku CLI.

3. Create a new app in the Heroku dashboard or via the CLI (heroku create).

4. Push your app to Heroku using Git:

```bash
```

```
git push heroku main
```

Heroku will automatically detect your app's dependencies (e.g., from requirements.txt) and install them.

4.5. Setting Up DigitalOcean for Python Deployment

1. Create a DigitalOcean account at https://digitalocean.com.

2. Launch a **Droplet**, which is essentially a virtual server, with a Python-friendly OS (Ubuntu is common).

3. SSH into the server and install Python, web servers like **Nginx** and **Gunicorn**, and set up your environment.

4. Deploy your code either by cloning a Git repository or transferring files via **SFTP**.

5. Deploying a Python Web Application to Heroku

5.1. Prerequisites for Heroku Deployment

Ensure you have the following set up:

- **Python** (specified in runtime.txt).

- **requirements.txt** for dependencies.

- **Procfile** to specify how Heroku should run your app (e.g., web: gunicorn app:app for Flask).

- **Heroku CLI** installed and authenticated.

5.2. Setting Up a Heroku Account and Installing the CLI

Follow the steps in the Heroku documentation to set up an account and install the CLI.

5.3. Deploying with Git and Heroku

1. Initialize a Git repository (if you haven't already):

```bash
git init
git add .
```

git commit -m "Initial commit"

2. Link your repository to Heroku:

bash

```
heroku create
```

3. Push the code to Heroku:

bash

```
git push heroku main
```

Heroku will automatically detect the environment (Python) and start the app.

5.4. Debugging Heroku Deployment Issues

If you encounter issues, use the following command to view logs:

bash

```
heroku logs --tail
```

5.5. Adding a Database on Heroku

Heroku provides **PostgreSQL** databases as part of its service. To add a database:

bash

```
heroku addons:create heroku-postgresql:hobby-dev
```

Heroku will provide you with a **DATABASE_URL** environment variable, which you can use in your app to connect to the database.

5.6. Scaling and Managing Dynos on Heroku

Heroku allows you to scale your app by adding or removing **dynos** (containers running your app):

```
bash
```

```
heroku ps:scale web=2
```

This command scales your web process to 2 dynos.

---

6. Deploying a Python Web Application to DigitalOcean

6.1. Understanding DigitalOcean's Infrastructure

DigitalOcean uses **Droplets**, which are simple virtual private servers (VPS) that run on Linux. Droplets are great for Python apps because you have complete control over the configuration.

6.2. Setting Up a Droplet and Configuring Your Server

1. Create a Droplet in the DigitalOcean dashboard.

2. SSH into your Droplet:

bash

```
ssh root@your_droplet_ip
```

6.3. Installing and Configuring Python and Web Servers

On your server, install Python and a web server like **Gunicorn**:

bash

```
sudo apt update
sudo apt install python3-pip python3-dev libpq-dev
pip3 install gunicorn
```

You'll also need to set up **Nginx** to serve your app.

6.4. Deploying Your Python Web App to DigitalOcean

You can transfer your code to DigitalOcean via **Git** or **SFTP**. Once your code is on the server, set up Gunicorn to run your app and configure Nginx to forward requests to it.

6.5. Setting Up Databases and Networking on DigitalOcean

For databases, you can either use **PostgreSQL** or **MySQL** and set them up on the same droplet or use managed databases. Configure your **database connection strings** and make sure your firewall is properly configured.

6.6. Scaling Your Application on DigitalOcean

DigitalOcean makes it easy to scale your app by adding more **Droplets** or using **Kubernetes** for containerized applications.

---

7. Maintaining Your Web Application

7.1. Debugging and Error Handling in Production

- Always log errors and track them with services like **Sentry** or **Loggly**.

- Use **remote debugging tools** like **PyCharm** for Python to inspect and debug production issues.

7.2. Monitoring Performance and Availability

Use tools like **New Relic**, **Datadog**, or **Prometheus** to monitor your app's performance in real-time. These tools track response times, resource usage, and availability.

7.3. Setting Up Logs and Alerts

Configure **log aggregation services** such as **Loggly** or **Elastic Stack** to collect logs and send alerts on certain events.

7.4. Handling Web Traffic and Load Balancing

For high-traffic apps, use **load balancers** to distribute incoming traffic across multiple servers or dynos. DigitalOcean and AWS offer managed load balancing services to handle this for you.

---

8. Security Best Practices for Deployed Web Apps

8.1. Using HTTPS and SSL Certificates

Always use **SSL/TLS encryption** for secure communication between your server and users' browsers. Tools like **Let's Encrypt** provide free SSL certificates.

8.2. Database Security and Data Encryption

Ensure that sensitive data (like passwords and financial information) is encrypted in the database. Use libraries like **bcrypt** to hash passwords and **SSL** to encrypt database connections.

8.3. Preventing Unauthorized Access with Firewalls

Configure your **firewall** to block unauthorized access to your server. Use tools like **ufw** (Uncomplicated Firewall) to secure your server.

8.4. Regular Updates and Patch Management

Ensure your server and software are always up-to-date. Regularly run security patches to avoid exploits in outdated software.

---

9. Scaling Your Web Application

9.1. Vertical vs. Horizontal Scaling

- **Vertical scaling** involves adding more resources (RAM, CPU) to your existing server.

- **Horizontal scaling** involves adding more servers (or droplets), spreading the load across multiple machines.

9.2. Using Load Balancers to Distribute Traffic

Load balancers can distribute traffic across multiple instances of your app, ensuring optimal performance under high loads.

9.3. Auto-Scaling in Cloud Environments

Many cloud providers like **AWS** and **DigitalOcean** offer auto-scaling features that automatically increase or decrease server capacity based on traffic demand.

9.4. Database Scaling and Replication

For large-scale applications, consider **database replication** to distribute the load. Use master-slave configurations where the master handles writes, and slaves handle read requests.

---

10. Real-World Example: Deploying Your Final Project

10.1. Overview of the Project: A Python-Powered Web App

Let's assume you've built a Flask or Django application that collects user data and displays it in a dashboard. We will deploy this app to both **Heroku** and **DigitalOcean** for a comprehensive deployment experience.

10.2. Preparing the App for Deployment

- Clean up your code, remove debug logs, and configure the environment for production.

- Set up requirements.txt and Procfile for Heroku.

10.3. Deploying to Heroku: Step-by-Step Walkthrough

- Follow the Heroku CLI setup steps mentioned earlier.

- Push your code to Heroku using Git.

- Add a **PostgreSQL** database to your Heroku app.

10.4. Deploying to DigitalOcean: Step-by-Step Walkthrough

- Set up a droplet on DigitalOcean.

- SSH into your server and install all necessary dependencies.

- Push your app code to the droplet via Git or SFTP.

10.5. Final Testing and Post-Deployment Actions

Once deployed, test all features to ensure they work as expected. Make sure the app is responsive, secure, and fully functional.

---

11. Conclusion

Deploying and maintaining a Python-powered web app requires careful planning, robust security, and consistent monitoring. Whether you choose **Heroku** for its simplicity or **DigitalOcean** for

more flexibility, both platforms offer powerful tools for deployment. Regular maintenance—including monitoring, scaling, and security updates—ensures your web app remains performant and secure over time. By following best practices, you can deploy with confidence and focus on building the next great feature of your application.